Palgrave Studies in Political Marketing and Management

Series Editor
Jennifer Lees-Marshment, School of Social Science, Politics and International Relations, University of Auckland, Auckland, New Zealand

Palgrave Studies in Political Marketing and Management (PalPMM) series publishes high quality and ground-breaking academic research on this growing area of government and political behaviour that attracts increasing attention from scholarship, teachers, the media and the public. It covers political marketing intelligence including polling, focus groups, role play, co-creation, segmentation, voter profiling, stakeholder insight; the political consumer; political management including crisis management, change management, issues management, reputation management, delivery management; political advising; political strategy such as positioning, targeting, market-orientation, political branding; political leadership in all its many different forms and arena; political organization including managing a political office, political HR, internal party marketing; political communication management such as public relations and e-marketing and ethics of political marketing and management.

For more information email the series editor Jennifer Lees-Marshment on j.lees-marshment@auckland.ac.nz and see https://leesmarshment.wordpress.com/pmm-book-series/.

Jamie Gillies · Vincent Raynauld ·
André Turcotte
Editors

Political Marketing in the 2021 Canadian Federal Election

palgrave
macmillan

Editors
Jamie Gillies
Department of Journalism
and Communications
St. Thomas University
Fredericton, NB, Canada

Vincent Raynauld
Department of Communication
Studies
Emerson College
Boston, MA, USA

André Turcotte
School of Journalism
and Communication
Carleton University
Ottawa, ON, Canada

ISSN 2946-2614 ISSN 2946-2622 (electronic)
Palgrave Studies in Political Marketing and Management
ISBN 978-3-031-34403-9 ISBN 978-3-031-34404-6 (eBook)
https://doi.org/10.1007/978-3-031-34404-6

© The Editor(s) (if applicable) and The Author(s), under exclusive license to Springer Nature Switzerland AG 2023, corrected publication 2023

This work is subject to copyright. All rights are solely and exclusively licensed by the Publisher, whether the whole or part of the material is concerned, specifically the rights of translation, reprinting, reuse of illustrations, recitation, broadcasting, reproduction on microfilms or in any other physical way, and transmission or information storage and retrieval, electronic adaptation, computer software, or by similar or dissimilar methodology now known or hereafter developed.
The use of general descriptive names, registered names, trademarks, service marks, etc. in this publication does not imply, even in the absence of a specific statement, that such names are exempt from the relevant protective laws and regulations and therefore free for general use.
The publisher, the authors, and the editors are safe to assume that the advice and information in this book are believed to be true and accurate at the date of publication. Neither the publisher nor the authors or the editors give a warranty, expressed or implied, with respect to the material contained herein or for any errors or omissions that may have been made. The publisher remains neutral with regard to jurisdictional claims in published maps and institutional affiliations.

This Palgrave Macmillan imprint is published by the registered company Springer Nature Switzerland AG
The registered company address is: Gewerbestrasse 11, 6330 Cham, Switzerland

Contents

1. Introduction: The 2021 Canadian Federal Election — 1
   Vincent Raynauld, Jamie Gillies, and André Turcotte

2. Political Branding in a Crisis and the Shifting Strategies of the Trudeau 2021 Campaign — 9
   Jennifer Lees-Marshment and Salma Malik

3. Clowns to the Left of Me, Jokers to the Right: Branding Challenges in the 2021 Conservative Party Campaign — 25
   Jamie Gillies and Angela Wisniewski

4. The Hyper–Masculine Campaign: Party Leader Brand Image, Heteronormativity and the 2021 Canadian Federal Election — 41
   Mireille Lalancette and Vincent Raynauld

5. Le Bloc Québécois: A Niche Party — 73
   Guy Lachapelle

6. The People's Party of Canada and the Appeal of Anger Politics — 91
   André Turcotte, David Coletto, and Simon Vodrey

7	The Neglected Populists: Breaking Down the Performance of the Left-Leaning New Democratic Party in the 2021 Canadian Federal Election André Turcotte and Vincent Raynauld	113
8	Identity Marketing During the 2021 Canadian Federal Election Mireille Lalancette, Angelia Wagner, Karen Bird, and Joanna Everitt	133
9	Conclusion: The Calm Before the Storm Jamie Gillies, André Turcotte, and Vincent Raynauld	155
	Correction to: The People's Party of Canada and the Appeal of Anger Politics André Turcotte, David Coletto, and Simon Vodrey	C1
	Index	161

LIST OF CONTRIBUTORS

Karen Bird Department of Political Science, McMaster University, Hamilton, ON, Canada

David Coletto Abacus Data, Ottawa, ON, Canada

Joanna Everitt Department of History and Politics, University of New Brunswick Saint John, Saint John, NB, Canada

Jamie Gillies Department of Journalism and Communications, St. Thomas University, Fredericton, NB, Canada

Guy Lachapelle Department of Political Science, Concordia University, Montreal, QC, Canada

Mireille Lalancette Département de Lettres et Communication Sociale, Université du Québec à Trois-Rivières, Trois-Rivières, QC, Canada

Jennifer Lees-Marshment Department of Politics and International Relations, University of Auckland, Auckland, New Zealand

Salma Malik Department of Politics and International Relations, University of Auckland, Auckland, New Zealand

Vincent Raynauld Department of Communication Studies, Emerson College, Boston, MA, USA

André Turcotte School of Journalism and Communication, Carleton University, Ottawa, ON, Canada

Simon Vodrey School of Journalism and Communication, Carleton University, Ottawa, ON, Canada

Angelia Wagner Department of Political Science, University of Alberta, Edmonton, AB, Canada

Angela Wisniewski Department of Journalism and Communications, St. Thomas University, Fredericton, NB, Canada

List of Figures

Fig. 2.1	Criteria for a Prime Minister's brand in government (*Source* Lees-Marshment [2021], adapted from Needham [2005], Smith [2009], Barberio and Lowe [2006] and Langmaid [2012])	11
Fig. 2.2	The 2019 and 2021 Liberal-Trudeau brands	13
Fig. 2.3	Recommendations for practice	21
Fig. 4.1	Screenshot of an Instagram post on Erin O'Toole's personal account featuring an announcement from CPC campaign studios shared during the campaign	44
Fig. 4.2	CPC Party Platform Cover for the 2021 federal elections featured in an Instagram post by O'Toole on August 16, 2021	53
Fig. 4.3	Instagram Post showing O'Toole in action when he was an army pilot published during the campaign	55
Fig. 4.4	Caption of an Instagram Post showing O'Toole in action when he was an army pilot published during the campaign	56
Fig. 4.5	Instagram Post showing O'Toole in action when he was an army pilot shared during the campaign	57
Fig. 4.6	Instagram post showing O'Toole in front of a Canada search and rescue helicopter shared during the campaign	58
Fig. 4.7	Instagram post showing O'Toole's campaign promises shared during the campaign	59
Fig. 4.8	Instagram post showing O'Toole promises posted during the campaign	60

Fig. 4.9	Caption of O'Toole Instagram account with the slogan secure the future posted during the campaign	61
Fig. 4.10	Instagram post picturing O'Toole jogging shared on during the campaign	62
Fig. 4.11	Instagram post picturing O'Toole with a cowboy hat	63
Fig. 4.12	Instagram post picturing O'Toole with his family advocating for the welfare of animals	64
Fig. 5.1	In the 2019 election, the Bloc Québécois made significant gains in the Greater Montreal area. In 2021, the Liberals needed to take a number of seats from the BQ to form a majority government (*Source* https://ici.radio-canada.ca/info/2019/elections-federales/resultats-cartes-vainqueur-perdant-partis-circonscriptions/)	80
Fig. 5.2	The leaders' tour during the 2019 federal election. Half of the events held by Yves-François Blanchet, the leader of the Bloc, took place in the greater Montreal area (*Source* https://ici.radio-canada.ca/info/2019/elections-federales/resultats-cartes-vainqueur-perdant-partis-circonscriptions/)	81
Fig. 5.3	Voting intention in Québec—September 14–17, 2021 (*Source* https://legermarketing.wpenginepowered.com/wp-content/uploads/2021/09/Rapport-politique-federale-18-sept-2021_VFinale-media.pdf)	85
Fig. 8.1	The Triangle of Leadership (*Source* Ceccobelli and Di Gregorio 2022: 118)	137

LIST OF TABLES

Table 5.1	Minority Governments in Canada	75
Table 5.2	The 38 proposals of the Bloc Québécois	78
Table 6.1	Demographic and socio-economic profile of People's Party supporters vs. other electors	108
Table 6.2	Views on the direction of Canada	108
Table 6.3	Feelings towards Justin Trudeau	109
Table 6.4	Position on COVID-19 vaccination	109
Table 6.5	Support for federal vaccine mandate	109
Table 6.6	Trust in other people	110
Table 7.1	Most important policy issue	125
Table 7.2	Words associated with NDP party leader Jagmeet Singh	127
Table 7.3	Words associated with LPC party leader Justin Trudeau	127
Table 7.4	Words associated with CPC party leader Erin O'Toole	128

CHAPTER 1

Introduction: The 2021 Canadian Federal Election

Vincent Raynauld, Jamie Gillies, and André Turcotte

Abstract The 2021 Canadian election was a unique experience as a campaign delivered under the constraints of a global pandemic. This chapter provides an overview of the book and considers how this election fits within the evolution of political marketing and branding in Canada.

Keywords Election · Canadian politics · Marketing · Branding · Trudeau

V. Raynauld (✉)
Department of Communication Studies, Emerson College, Boston, MA, USA
e-mail: vincent_raynauld@emerson.edu

J. Gillies
Department of Journalism and Communications, St. Thomas University, Fredericton, NB, Canada
e-mail: jgillies@stu.ca

A. Turcotte
School of Journalism and Communication, Carleton University, Ottawa, ON, Canada
e-mail: andre.turcotte@carleton.ca

© The Author(s), under exclusive license to Springer Nature Switzerland AG 2023
J. Gillies et al. (eds.), *Political Marketing in the 2021 Canadian Federal Election*, Palgrave Studies in Political Marketing and Management, https://doi.org/10.1007/978-3-031-34404-6_1

1

Prime Minister Justin Trudeau's August 2021 decision to call a snap election in a second attempt to form a majority government in less than three years demonstrated the importance and centrality of dynamics of electioneering and political marketing. Regardless of polls or apt conditions to send voters to the polls, parties and their leaders still have to go on the campaign trail during the writ period to defend their records (in the case of incumbents), introduce and promote their policy proposals and contrast them with those of their opponents, showcase their readiness to assume or keep political office, as well as mobilize voters and secure their support ahead of Election Day. In many ways, political campaigns often matter more than the political and policy priorities of the day, or the prevailing sentiments shaping voters' political attitudes as the campaign sheds light on issues with new saliency. Those campaign issues often lead the way and result in anachronistic results and surprises.

Such was the case with the 2021 Canadian federal election. While the Liberal Party of Canada (LPC) and its leader—Justin Trudeau— won the contest, it was only able to secure a minority government mandate similar to the one they had achieved in 2019. While the previous campaign had been marred by personal attacks and an overt emphasis on Trudeau's personality and shortcomings (e.g., CBC News 2019), this 2021 electoral contest was marked by a different public political discourse, as discussed in the different chapters in this book. Specifically, as different facets of Canadian society were still impacted by the COVID-19 global pandemic and the public health measures deployed by local, regional and national governments to limit its effects, significant attention was given to policies related to healthcare. In many ways, this incited many parties and their leaders to adjust their approach and reposition their political and policy offerings. For example, under the new leadership of Erin O'Toole who was elected in this position on August 23, 2020, Conservative Party of Canada's (CPC) policy positions on a wide range of social issues tacked to the centre—or left-of-centre—in the hopes of winning over a large swath of the Canadian electorate who were concerned about the uncertainty caused by the COVID-19 pandemic (see chapter by Lalancette and Raynauld). Jagmeet Singh's New Democratic Party (NDP) took up left-wing populist sentiment on environmental, social and labour justice issues, moving into the gap vacated by the Green Party of Canada in trying to offer a progressive alternative to the Liberals. Benefiting from a popular soft sovereigntist premier in François Legault who supported the CPC in the election, the Bloc Quebecois (BQ) positioned itself as an effective voice for Quebecers in Ottawa. Finally, the People's Party of Canada (PPC) led by Maxime Bernier capitalized on a small but vocal and ardent group of voters who opposed Canada's pandemic response—including the lockdowns and different public health mandates—and presented itself as the protest populist alternative to the CPC.

Throughout the month-long campaign, attempts at rebranding, targeted marketing and, in the case of Quebec, targeted voter outreach and engagement techniques tailored to the social, linguistic and cultural specificity of that province, were used to mobilize members of the public so they would turn out and vote in the context of an election unwanted by a large swath of the Canadian electorate. Despite the outcome being similar to 2019, this edited collection spotlights a wide range of political marketing strategies, phenomena and techniques that marked the approach to electioneering of many candidates and political parties, especially in the wake of other COVID-19-era elections such as the 2020 U.S. presidential elections. In many ways, the Canadian case offers a microcosm of the kinds of enduring political marketing that wind up spanning the globe. The 2021 electoral contest marked a transitional moment for Canada, both in terms of political discourse and how parties and leaders will likely shift in their marketing and branding. For a variety of reasons, Canada had resisted contemporary populist impulses, with the major parties eschewing sops and appeals to alt-right, far-right and far-left forces. But in 2021, those populist voices found a home with the PPC and that split the vote on the right for the first time since the 2000s. After O'Toole and the CPC's defeat, Pierre Poilievre—who was elected CPC leader on September 10, 2022—gained traction in the Canadian political landscape by going after voters on the right of the political spectrum. To some degree, it could mark an important shift in marketing and branding that may play itself out in future elections and position Canada more in line with other Western democracies that have been impacted by these populist forces.

As mentioned previously, this book is of particular importance as it examines the political marketing strategies and techniques deployed by political parties and candidates in the context of an election during a worldwide pandemic. In many ways, the uncertainty caused by the spread and effects of the SARS-CoV-2 virus internationally forced them to rethink and adjust their usual political marketing playbook. This edited collection also addresses—directly and indirectly—some facets of the Freedom Convoy movement that followed in early 2022 and the subsequent CPC leadership campaign in which Poilievre won a landslide victory after O'Toole was removed as leader. Much like the 2020 U.S. presidential contest, the marketing and branding narrative did not end on Election Day, especially in the context of 24/7 campaigning.

This edited volume brings together an international and interdisciplinary team of practitioners and scholars with a diverse range of expertise and perspectives to unpack the campaign from various political marketing angles. Specifically, the contributors to this book offer theoretical, methodological and more practical insights from different angles, including polling, gender studies, marketing, political communication and health and science communication. This comprises chapters that attempt to dissect the various political marketing and branding themes that came about in the 2021 federal election. Some of these themes are a continued narrative about brands and particular marketing styles, while others suggest innovative ways in which parties, leaders and regions connected with the public. It continues the recent exploration of elections and political marketing and branding that have garnered new foci and ways of looking at the impact of these events.

This edited collection builds on and inserts itself into a stream of academic works that have taken a deep dive in different facets of political communication, marketing and electioneering at the local, regional and national levels in Canada. Of particular importance are Alex Marland, Thierry Giasson and Jennifer Lees-Marshment's edited volume (2012) which provided one of the first holistic looks at political marketing in the Canadian context. In 2015, Marland and Giasson edited a collection analysing the 2015 Canadian federal election from a wide range of perspectives. More recently, Marland and Giasson's (2020) edited volume on the management of campaigns in Canada comprised chapters resulting from collaborations between scholars and practitioners who explored different aspects of the political communication, marketing and management activities of political parties and candidates during elections. Lastly, Marland and Giasson (2022: 20) spearheaded a project taking interest in "local-level campaign activities within a Canadian federal election", from campaign signage to voter canvassing and election administration. It should be noted that many other academic works exploring specific facets of political marketing have been published over the last decade, including Gillies et al. (2020), McGrane (2019), Marland (2016, 2018),

Turcotte (2020), as well as Marland et al. (2017). Internationally, a wealth of books and other academic publications exploring dynamics of political marketing in different national contexts have been published. Of note are works by Dobscha (2019), Elder and Lees-Marshment (2021), Mensah (2017) and Gillies (2017, 2022).

This book is structured as follows. In the second chapter, the University of Auckland's Jennifer Lees-Marshment and Salma Malik look at Trudeau's branding in the 2021 election through the lens of crisis politics amidst the pandemic. Their chapter considers how Trudeau's team shifted the brand from an intense focus on Trudeau personally to one that structured the brand around the Liberal government's pandemic response and the relative weakness of the CPC and NDP to provide coherent governance in the crisis. But it also suggests the limitations with crisis-inspired branding, particularly with an electorate tired of lockdowns and mandates. Trudeau, for all of his political brand advantages from the 2015 campaign—young, dynamic, hope and change—did not gain any traction from the Canadian government's response to the pandemic. This is despite polling throughout 2020 and 2021 that consistently showed the vast majority of the public supportive of the Trudeau government's efforts to manage COVID-19.

In the third chapter, Jamie Gillies and Angela Wisniewski from St. Thomas University consider Erin O'Toole's campaign to rebrand himself and the CPC in the 2021 election. They consider the origins, consequences and fallout of the O'Toole rebrand attempts. In the first half of the election campaign which was marked by Trudeau and the Liberals experiencing some political outreach and engagement difficulties, the CPC had an opportunity to position themselves strategically in order to gain traction among some segments of the public and win the election. Instead, O'Toole seemed to tack too far to the centre, even centre-left and left himself and the party open to attacks that he was not a "true blue conservative". The campaign then sputtered amidst attacks on policy positions. O'Toole's branding tactics should have appealed to middle of the road voters, especially in the suburbs that the CPC needed to win back. Instead, the campaign was no better than the previous election. The chapter also considers the CPC rebrand under Pierre Poilievre which occurred almost immediately following the election, amidst the Freedom Convoy protest movement in Ottawa—and in other localities across Canada—and the embrace by the party of right-wing populism.

In the fourth chapter, Mireille Lalancette and Vincent Raynauld examine the mobilization of hypermasculine political communication and marketing strategies by party leaders during the 2021 election. Their chapter analyses O'Toole's Instagram posts during the campaign as well as other digital marketing materials to consider messaging techniques filtered through the lens of hypermasculinity. Most notably, they take an interest in O'Toole's deliberate marketing of his image as the "man with the plan". It also codes direct and indirect appeals to masculinity to explore identity-based uses of social media in political marketing campaigns.

In the fifth chapter, Guy Lachapelle analyses the province of Quebec from a political branding standpoint and in particular looks at how the Bloc Québécois used the key themes of autonomy from Ottawa and the popularity of the Coalition avenir Québec (CAQ) government to differentiate it from the Trudeau Liberals. His chapter, Le Bloc Québécois: A Niche Party, Quebec as a province is seen as integral to almost every Canadian election campaign and usually determines whether the LPC or CPC forms a majority government. 2021 was no exception. Yves-François Blanchet's party was able to effectively block both the Liberals and the CPC from making inroads into Quebec by nationalizing the Quebec provincial brand during the campaign.

In the sixth chapter, André Turcotte, David Coletto and Simon Vodrey examine the appeal of the PPC in the 2021 election amidst the pandemic by considering how its leader Maxime Bernier marketed the party with little grassroots organization and money. Their chapter, The People's Party of Canada and the Appeal of Anger Politics, considers the role of anger in how the PPC motivated voters and, alternatively, how voters motivated the PPC to focus on anger. They use extensive polling research to see how anger politics appealed to voters and helped right-wing and far-right populism to go mainstream in Canada.

In the seventh chapter, Turcotte and Raynauld consider left-wing populism in Canada in the context of the 2021 election, addressing a literature gap in political marketing. Their chapter, The Neglected Populists: Breaking Down the Performance of the Left-Leaning New Democratic Party in the 2021 Canadian Federal Election, uses national surveys conducted during the election to consider left-wing populist political markets and how well the NDP and Jagmeet Singh leveraged this voting bloc that is often ignored or considered too diffuse on which to expend political capital to influence.

In the eighth chapter, Mireille Lalancette, Angelia Wagner, Karen Bird and Joanna Everitt look at the identity marketing strategies of candidates during the 2021 Canadian federal election. Their chapter, Identity Marketing During the 2021 Canadian Federal Election, analyses official candidate biographies and identifies the strategies utilized to address their immigration status in political marketing. This builds on their work on mediatization and personalization of candidates by adding a political marketing dimension. This chapter reveals that challengers use their immigration stories to demonstrate a commitment to community and country, while incumbents, high-profile individuals and second- or third-generation Canadians downplay their immigration background in favour of emphasizing their skills and qualifications.

By offering an edited collection with a mix of political science and communications researchers as well as political marketing experts, this book makes two major contributions to the academic and professional literature: (1) consider how Canadian leaders and parties met the political environment of 2021 and 2022 in terms of marketing and branding, especially with respect to engaging voters and supporters; (2) recognize that brand endurance and current marketing trends are likely to undergo a major shift in Canada as populism is embraced and mainstreamed into the politics of a number of the parties. This collection outlines those distinctly Canadian political trends and how they are interacting with broader and more global political marketing and branding trends.

References

CBC News (2019). What we know about Justin Trudeau's blackface photos—And what happens next. *CBC News*. https://www.cbc.ca/news/politics/canada-votes-2019-trudeau-blackface-brownface-cbc-explains-1.5290664.

Dobscha, S. (2019). *Handbook of research on gender and marketing*. Edward Elgar Publishing.

Elder, Edward and Jennifer Lees-Marshment (Eds.). (2021). *Political marketing and management in the 2020 New Zealand general election*. London: Springer Nature.

Gillies, Jamie (Ed.). (2017). *Political marketing in the 2016 U.S. presidential election*. London: Palgrave Pivot.

Gillies, Jamie (Ed.). (2022). *Political marketing in the 2020 U.S. presidential election*. London: Palgrave Pivot.

Gillies, Jamie, Vincent Raynauld and André Turcotte (Eds.). (2020) *Political marketing in the 2019 Canadian federal election*. London: Palgrave Pivot.

Marland, Alex. (2016). *Brand command: Canadian politics and democracy in the age of message control*. Vancouver: UBC Press.
Marland, Alex. (2018). The brand image of Canadian Prime Minister Justin Trudeau in international context. *Canadian Foreign Policy Journal*, 24(2), 139–144
Marland, Alex, Thierry Giasson and Jennifer Lees-Marshment (Eds.). (2012). *Political marketing in Canada*. Vancouver: UBC Press.
Marland, Alex and Thierry Giasson (Eds.). (2015). *Canadian election analysis 2015: Communication, strategy and democracy*. Samara Canada and UBC Press. Digital Publication.
Marland, Alex and Thierry Giasson (Eds.). (2020). *Inside the campaign: Managing elections in Canada*. Vancouver: UBC Press.
Marland, Alex and Thierry Giasson (Eds.). (2022). *Inside the local campaign: Constituency elections in Canada*. Vancouver: UBC Press.
Marland, Alex, J.P. Lewis and Tom Flanagan. (2017). Governance in the age of digital media and branding. *Governance*, 30(1), 125–141.
McGrane, D. (2019). *The new NDP: Moderation, modernization, and political marketing*. Vancouver: UBC Press.
Mensah, Kobby (Ed.) (2017). *Political marketing and management in Ghana: A new architecture*. London: Springer Nature.
Turcotte, André. (2020). *Political marketing alchemy: The state of opinion research*. London: Springer Nature.

CHAPTER 2

Political Branding in a Crisis and the Shifting Strategies of the Trudeau 2021 Campaign

Jennifer Lees-Marshment and Salma Malik

Abstract This chapter will explore the branding of Prime Minister Justin Trudeau in the 2021 campaign and the lessons from this for political branding in a crisis. It explains how the 2021 Liberal-Trudeau brand was visibly impacted by the COVID-19 pandemic. It was focused on the present, safety and protection, and while it retained an environmental focus it downplayed the part of Justin Trudeau himself while highlighting the weaknesses of the opposition. This did little to inspire voters already tired of living in a pandemic for nearly two years and support for Trudeau declined significantly between the call of the election and the final vote. The chapter therefore highlighted the challenges of political branding in a

J. Lees-Marshment (✉) · S. Malik
Department of Politics and International Relations,
University of Auckland, Auckland, New Zealand
e-mail: j.lees-marshment@auckland.ac.nz

S. Malik
e-mail: smal291@aucklanduni.ac.nz

© The Author(s), under exclusive license to Springer Nature Switzerland AG 2023
J. Gillies et al. (eds.), *Political Marketing in the 2021 Canadian Federal Election*, Palgrave Studies in Political Marketing and Management,
https://doi.org/10.1007/978-3-031-34404-6_2

crisis and generates lessons both for Trudeau and political leaders around the world.

Keywords Political branding · Brand personality · Trudeau · Liberal · Government branding · Crisis · Strategy

Introduction

Political branding is a vital activity in political marketing both to win power and maintain it. Trudeau used political branding successfully to win in 2015 and to get re-elected in 2019. However, the longer leaders are in power the more challenging it gets as unpredictable events and crises make it hard for leaders to deliver their promised brand. The COVID-19 pandemic created an unprecedented challenge to brand maintenance for all leaders around the world. This chapter will review the effectiveness of the Liberal and Trudeau brand offered in 2021 and the implications for Trudeau going forward and more widely branding leaders during a crisis.

Literature, Theoretical Framework and Methodology

Political branding is a major area of political marketing. Brands are important to convey an overall sense of what a leader and party are about, and most importantly, what they are offering to voters for the future. Previous research has demonstrated that leaders, their government and their policies need to convey certain characteristics to win election and re-election. For example, leaders need to show competent leadership, convey honesty and be unique in some way to maintain support from voters. The government needs to offer a simple and aspirational brand so voters have a strong sense of how they will improve their lives in the future and that they are capable of delivering on promises. Policies need to use universal values and long-term benefits. Fulfilling these criteria is especially important for a leader seeking a third term, who—as was the case for Trudeau—may have been tarnished by failed delivery or scandal during their time in power. An effective brand is important to make clear to voters why it is worth voting for them again.

This chapter will use criteria from the same theoretical framework used in the analysis of Trudeau's brand in 2019 (Lees-Marshment 2021) which combines understanding from multiple theories (see Fig. 2.1) to explore how well Trudeau met key branding criteria. Over 250 primary data sources were reviewed for the 2021 campaign period, August 15 when parliament was dissolved to September 20, from the Liberal Party platform, Liberal Party Media releases, Liberal Party YouTube, Liberal Party Facebook advertising, Justin Trudeau's Facebook and public polls. This data was thematically coded as to the extent to which it met such principles. The analysis assessed both text and images. Opinion poll data was also reviewed for information about how the public perceived the brand.

Leaders brand personality
• **Honest**: reliable, wholesome, sincere, real, down to earth
• **Spirited image**: daring, imaginative, up to date, trendy, cheerful, cool, contemporary
• **Leadership**: competent, intelligence, successful, hardworking, secure
• **Toughness**: masculine, tough, outdoorsy, rugged
• **Uniqueness**: original, different, unique, independent
Government brand effectiveness
• **Simple**: make it easy for voters to understand what is on offer
• **Aspirational**: convey a positive vision for a better way of life
• **Differentiated**: make the differences between the brand and the competition clear
• **Credible**: convey the government is capable of delivering reasonable promises, and reassure voters it is not risky to support the brand
• **Symbolic**: convey positive values
Policy branding
• **Appeal to universally desired values** and key phrases that resonate with voters and their values
• **Claim the competition's brand lacks these values**
• **Convey broader benefits beyond specific policies**
Rebranding
• **Rebrand and reconnect**: acknowledge leader mistakes and do a listening tour
• **Use co-creation research to identify solutions to a leaders declining brand**: ask the public how they would like the leader to behave
• **Expand the brand beyond the leader**: show the overall team

Fig. 2.1 Criteria for a Prime Minister's brand in government (*Source* Lees-Marshment [2021], adapted from Needham [2005], Smith [2009], Barberio and Lowe [2006] and Langmaid [2012])

The Liberal and Trudeau Branding in the 2021 Election Campaign

Political branding in the 2021 election was unusual for two reasons: one it was held during the extended COVID-19 crisis, and two the election was called only two years after the last one. Superficially this seemed sensible as Trudeau and the Liberals were doing well in the polls. However, it cut short the time available to deliver 2019 brand promises and gave political marketing advisors little time to redesign the brand for the new market conditions caused by COVID-19 where impacts extended beyond physical health to mental health, the economy and education. As the analysis will show, the 2021 brand effectiveness was mixed and the election result was not strong.

The Canadian Liberal Party's 2021 Brand: Safety First

The 2021 brand was all about the short term and safety first. It dropped key elements from the 2019 brand. As Fig. 2.2 shows, 2019 was all about future-oriented action, climate change action for the economy, tax cuts for families, positive investment in children, led by a spirited and youth-oriented Trudeau and clearly distinct from an opposition that was going backwards (see Lees-Marshment 2021). However, in 2021 it was more present-oriented, led by a leader working together with Canadians, focused on fair home ownership, green jobs and protecting children. The one brand element retained and even strengthened was being distinct to the opposition by portraying a sense of safety in contrast to a dangerous, backward-looking Conservative Party.

Overall this meant aspiration was lacking in 2021, with more focus on undermining the opposition and the need for safety and protection. It failed to give voters a sense of future direction or motivation to get out to vote for Trudeau.

Leaders Brand Personality

The leader component of the brand was rarely seen—even on Trudeau's own Facebook page, he was mostly in the background or focusing on other people around such as his team and voters. Liberal Party ads focused more on policy than leadership.

2 POLITICAL BRANDING IN A CRISIS AND THE SHIFTING ... 13

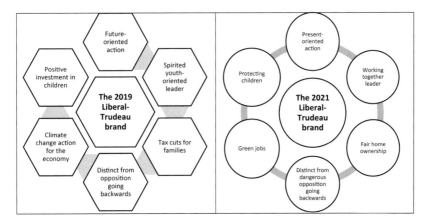

Fig. 2.2 The 2019 and 2021 Liberal-Trudeau brands

Honesty, which includes being reliable and down to earth, was only conveyed a few times. One ad featured Trudeau's comments when looking directly at the camera at the English leader's debate: "I made a promise during this pandemic to have people's backs. Every time I came out of my house to talk directly to Canadians I told them I'd be there for you" (Liberal Ad 2021 September 10). Trudeau was seen with a diverse range of voters (Trudeau 2021 August 16a, August 17, September 19a) and attempted to connect with them by acknowledging the challenges everyone had faced, noting that:

> The last 18 months have been incredibly challenging. They've been utterly exhausting. Hard on our kids, hard on our aging parents, and teachers, and frontline health workers, hard on everyone. (Liberal Youtube 2021 September 20)

A spirited image was even more rarely seen apart from a video distributed at the end of the campaign when videos showed him bounding up steps to go to speak to a crowd in the night, in a leather jacket and jeans, accompanied by a fast beat soundtrack (Liberal Youtube 2021 September 18a, 18b and 20).

Leadership competence was also mostly absent apart from a few Facebook posts where Trudeau talked about working with territories and provinces (Trudeau, Justin 2021 August 15) and towards the end of the campaign when he declared "I know where I stand, and my friends, it's with you" (Liberal Youtube 2021 September 20). There was no reminder of professional strengths, such as Trudeau working hard as Prime Minister during the pandemic.

Toughness was more strongly present but not always successful. At the start of the campaign in a video titled *Relentless* Trudeau discussed fighting for the country: "That's the Canada I know, and the Canada I fight for each and every day" (Liberal Youtube 2021 August 15a). It was also sometimes displayed through images of Trudeau in factories (Trudeau 2021 August 30) or using a drill (Trudeau 2021 September 19b) and through a strong tone when he spoke at an event in the final days of the campaign (Trudeau 2021 September 19c). However Facebook ads mostly featured a more rigid autocratic form of strength. One quoted Trudeau saying no to allowing people without a medical reason for not getting vaccinated to board a plane or train with accommodations (Liberal Ad 2021 August 23). Another ad featured a steadfast quote: "I am not going to back down, no matter how many of them show up to try and shout us down" (Liberal Ad 2021 September 16a).

Trudeau's previous brand uniqueness of gender all but disappeared in 2021, replaced with a partnership type leadership with talk of having worked hard together (Liberal Youtube 2021 August 15b), moving forward together (Liberal Youtube 2021 September 11) and images of Trudeau working with people (Liberal Youtube 2021 August 15a). The working together theme was also strong in Facebook advertising. Seven ads showing him among other people, working with them and listening to them and Trudeau saying "we worked as a team to keep our loved ones healthy and safe…we pulled together when it was needed the most … let's keep working to keep things together" (Liberal Ad 2021 August 24).

Government Brand Effectiveness

The Liberal brand was communicated more extensively than Trudeau's leadership, but its effectiveness was mixed.

It was simple and easy to understand as there was one core focus: safety. The Liberals emphasized that they had a "Plan to keep Canadians safe" (Liberal Media Release 2021 August 28) and would "protect Canadians" (Liberal Media Release 2021 August 28). Advertising made claims such as "Putting our healthcare workers' safety first is key" (Liberal Ad 2021 September 7a) and general "We'll continue to do whatever it takes to keep Canadians safe and supported" (Liberal Ad 2021 September 7b). Ten ads focused on seniors, discussing themes such as increased benefits, better care and giving safety and comfort. Another policy issue most frequently discussed in the Facebook ads was health, with 20 ads focused on health topics such as virtual health care, 10 days of sick leave and access to doctors and surgeries.

However, focusing on safety prevented the brand being seen as aspirational. While at the start of the campaign, there was more ambition with Trudeau saying "This is a big country, with big ideas" and "Let's think even bigger, Canada" accompanied by images of fast-moving traffic (Liberal Youtube 2021 August 15b and Liberal Ads 2021 August 29), this theme was dropped by early September. Discussions of home ownership were positive but not ambitious—"Let's make housing fair and affordable" (Liberal Youtube 2021 August 25, 29ab) did not evoke a vision for a better way of life. It was more about restoring what people had experienced previously.

Credibility was mixed. They did try to make the brand reassuring and low risk to vote for by reminding voters of the support the Liberal Government provided during the pandemic—"we helped workers and businesses keep their head above water" and distribute vaccines (Liberal Youtube 2021 August 15b). A positive ad in mid-August reminded voters of the achievements since being first elected in 2015 and gave new clear promises if re-elected (Liberal Ad 2021 August 16). They also tried to build credibility with 6 ads quoting positive external assessments of their economic policies, with images of either Trudeau and his team or the Minister of Finance, and targeted at the older age groups 55–64 and 65 plus (Liberal Ad 2021 September 15a). They also emphasized the affordability of their climate change plans, with a blitz of ads 7–8 and 15–16 September which cited expert endorsement of its affordability, noting that "According to analysis by Simon Fraser University's Mark Jaccard, the Liberals have the most effective and affordable plan, followed by the Conservatives, the Greens and, in a distant fourth, the NDP" (Liberal Ad 2021 September 15b) while another used the phrase "Liberals: A- for ambition, A- for feasibility" (Liberal Ad 2021 September 15c). Ads also emphasized past achievements: "it deserves credit for being the first federal government in Canada to meet (in fact exceed) its climate policy commitments" (Liberal Ad 2021 September 16b) and another that "in the past six years, the current Liberal government has done more to tackle climate change than previous governments did in over 20 years" (Liberal Ad 2021 September 15d).

However while they frequently talked about their plans—a "groundbreaking plan" on housing (Trudeau 2021 August 25), "a bold, progressive, ambitious plan to move Canada Forward" (Trudeau 2021 September 18) and a "real plan" in relation to climate change policies (Liberal Youtube 2021 September 17), there was little detail about such plans. In their policy platform, while some promises were specific—"10 days of paid sick leave for federally regulated workers" and "End plastic waste by 2030"—many were vague—"Better care in long-term care" and "Create green jobs in communities across Canada" (Liberal Party 2021). And videos about Liberal plans to help people buy a home often showed images of more costly housing despite their schemes targeting first-time home buyers (Liberal Youtube 2021 August 29a).

There were nevertheless two clear strengths: symbolism and differentiation. In terms of being symbolic of positive values, there were very frequent discussions and images of Canadians working together which were also connected to Canadian values. For example, in one video Trudeau said that "in Canada, we have each other's backs. We always have"—"We pull together to make things better—and leave no one behind" with images of Canadian landscapes, people and places throughout history, and modern but specifically Canadian images such as the flag in front of a tower block and a rainbow version of the flag in a LGBT parade (Liberal Youtube 2021 August 15a). In another, he talked about pulling together during the pandemic:

> Together we helped families and businesses get through the pandemic. And we worked as a team to keep our loved ones healthy and safe. We pulled together when it was needed the most. Let's keep working to make things better—and leave no one behind". (Liberal Youtube 2021 August 17)

This was combined Canadian imagery and Trudeau himself wearing a jacket with the maple leaf on the back (Liberal Youtube 2021 September 18a). There were also features of the positive impact of support the government gave to individuals during the pandemic (Liberal Youtube 2021 September 18c, d, e, f). Several ads in August reinforced this theme of working together, with ads featuring Trudeau repeating comments about having "each other's backs" and "we pull together" alongside images of Trudeau among others and people working together (Liberal

Ad 2021 August 15). However, this theme was not maintained—no ad on this theme was launched in September—undermining its effectiveness.

The biggest and most persistent brand theme was differentiation from the Conservatives. Multiple and frequent attempts to make the differences between the brand and the competition clear were evident in all data sources. They argued that the opposition wanted to adopt or return to positions that were unsafe in terms of vaccinations (Liberal Youtube 2021 August 29c), gun control and publicly funded health care (Liberal Youtube 2021 September 5a, b, c and 14), whereas the Liberals would protect "our kids" and ran a government that "always has your back" (Liberal Youtube 2021 September 18a). Media releases emphasized that "Erin O'Toole's Conservatives" would "take Canada backward" (Liberal Media release 2021 August 16). Differentiation was the most common and consistent theme in Facebook advertising, with nearly 50 ads differentiating the Liberals from the Conservative opposition. One ad included ordinary people saying what the Liberals would offer as opposed to the Conservatives, such as "enough vaccines for everyone" (Liberal Ad 2021 September 18a); others quoted external sources with higher rankings of the Liberal's climate plan compared with the Conservatives (Liberal Ad 2021 September 4) while another that the Liberals were "offering a much bolder plan" on housing than the other parties (Liberal Ad 2021 August 31). Others contrasted the two leaders on climate change, picturing Trudeau with the words "climate action" and O'Toole with "climate neglect" (Liberal Ad 2021 September 1). They also negatively branded the Conservatives as taking Canada backwards, using select but direct quotes from opposition leader Eric O'Toole (Liberal Ad 2021 September 18b).

Policy Branding

Policy branding was detectable in terms of appealing to universal values on vaccination and housing policy. Vaccination policies were framed in relation to protecting children with Trudeau declaring "I believe that vaccination should be mandatory for flying and taking trains to protect our children and ensure a return to normal" (Liberal Youtube 2021 August 29d and Liberal Youtube 2021 August 29c). And housing policy was very clearly discussed in terms of fairness. Trudeau claimed their plan would "crack down on unfair practices" and "make housing fair and affordable" (Liberal Youtube 2021 September 18g). There were 20 ads on housing, and these ads continued through to September and they emphasized fairness through arguments that policies would make homes more affordable and protect rights, with Trudeau arguing that they would help homes continue to be homes "where our families build a future together" (Liberal Ad 2021 September 14) while other ads emphasized the goal of "A home. For everyone" (Liberal Ad 2021 September 11) and included images of families and houses. They featured policies of a rent to own programme (Liberal Ad 2021 September 8), and a tax-free First Home Savings Account (FHSA) (Liberal Ad 2021 September 7c).

Rebranding

Given Trudeau's declining popularity it would have been very logical strategically to rebrand and reconnect the leader by showing the team more and getting in touch with voters. However branding did not focus on the team apart from when the campaign was launched (Liberal Media Release 2021 August 15; Trudeau 2021 August 16b) and a video that featured Quebec-based politicians who claimed to be "a team that speaks for Quebec, understands the priorities" (Liberal Youtube 2021 September 11). Nevertheless, on the September 1st, Trudeau started a country-wide bus tour to try to get in touch as well as convey a "working together" style of leadership, carried out a Facebook live where he answered questions sent in from voters (Trudeau 2021 September 12) and was also pictured listening to voters (Trudeau 2021 September 19d) but this was too late in the campaign to influence the overall brand.

Voter Perceptions of the Political Brand

Public polling explains the brand strategy used but also calls its effectiveness into question as it reveals similar strengths and weaknesses to analysis of party data.

Firstly, fairness was a value featured in polling results, with pre-campaign surveys showing that 70% wanted the federal government to work to build an economy and society that is more fair and equitable than it was before the pandemic (Abacus August 11, 2021, and Abacus 2021 August). The emphasis on the fairness of housing affordability in particular also aligns with voters' top four concerns which were cost of living, followed by health care, climate change and housing affordability (Abacus August 17, 2021, and Abacus September 2, 2021). Retaining a focus on climate change action but explaining how it was affordable aligns with polling that suggested it was a key issue for Liberal supporters (Abacus August 17, 2021) but voters at large worried about the cost of living. Had they dropped it, they could have created brand dissonance with their core supporters as happened with Australian PM Kevin Rudd when he reneged on climate change policy promises (Downer 2016). The focus of ads on health made sense as access to health care was an important issue to voters in surveys conducted before the campaign (Abacus August 25, 2021). Adding a focus on seniors through ads that emphasized safety also made sense as polls suggested that more senior voters were inclined towards voting for the Liberal Party (Ipsos September 15, 2021).

The downplaying or absence of Trudeau in the brand is logical given the breadth of data suggesting he was viewed negatively by voters. Abacus Data showed that 49% felt Mr. Trudeau was fake and 47% would describe him as untrustworthy, and this was worse than the Conservative and NDP leaders. (Abacus August 26, 2021). Ipsos data suggested that he was seen as most likely to "say anything to get elected", "has a hidden agenda", and "in over their head" (Ipsos September 4, 2021). Moreover, impressions of Trudeau got worse during the campaign, while other leaders' images improved (Abacus August 31, 2021) and Vote Compass (2021) data also showed he was seen as less trustworthy than in previous elections. The dropping of gender from his brand made tactical sense given that Trudeau was losing support among women in August 2021 and 41% were saying they viewed him "very unfavourably" (Angus Reid 2021 August 30).

Data shows that the Liberal brand was not seen as highly credible. Data indicated that voters' belief in the potential of the Liberals to make a difference in key areas was not high. On climate change, only 34% thought they would improve on the issue of reducing carbon emissions, only 24% improve access to health care and 18% housing affordability. Moreover, for those who prioritized health care, the Liberals were the preferred party of the two major contenders but only one-in-three (32%) said the Liberals would improve health care in a forthcoming term. Among those who say housing is a top priority, 22 per cent say the Liberals would improve the situation if they formed government, while 18 per cent say the Conservatives would (Angus Reid September 9, 2021). And data also showed that the Liberals only led on two of voters' top four concerns—health care and climate change—despite their emphasis on housing policy (Abacus August 17, 2021, and Abacus September 2, 2021).

Conclusion: Reflections on the 2021 Brand and Impact of the COVID-19 Crisis

The 2021 Liberal-Trudeau brand was a very constrained offering for Canadians and clearly impacted by the COVID-19 pandemic. It was much more focused on the present and safety than long-term aspiration and on seniors rather than youth. Although the brand emphasized values such as working together and fairness and retained an environmental focus, the affordability of policies had to be emphasized due to the cost of living crisis and its promised action on home ownership lacked credibility. Justin Trudeau's position in the brand was limited. The only brand element strengthened was being distinct to the opposition, by portraying a sense of safety in contrast to a dangerous, backward-looking Conservative Party. Overall, the 2021 brand lacked energy and did little to inspire voters already tired of living in a pandemic for nearly two years.

There was also a sense of a shifting brand strategy, where the initial ambitious talk for Canada apparent in early communication was displaced by an emphasis on safety, affordable rather than aspirational climate change policies and negative branding of the opposition. But this diverted attention away from what voters would receive from supporting the Liberal-Trudeau brand. Even discussion of values such as working together and fairness declined over the course of the campaign with no ads on working together launched in September. Additionally, unlike in New Zealand where the incumbent party focused their brand on their Prime Minister Jacinda Ardern and enjoyed a landslide victory in 2020 (Jalil 2021), the Liberals did not seem to know what to do with Justin Trudeau. Trudeau was not a feature for most of the campaign until a sudden change in tactics when he started a country-wide bus tour on September 1st. While we do recommend leaders in power try to reconnect and rebrand, doing so 16 days before the voting day is a bit late.

This resulted in a confused political brand, undermined the brand relationship between Trudeau and the Canadian public, and the election results were mixed. Substantial and significant rebranding is needed if the Liberals are to enjoy more success in the future—see Fig. 2.3.

In many ways, the deficiencies in political branding reflect the challenges created by an ever-extending and expanding crisis. As research on other countries has indicated, during a crisis the political market becomes unstable and unpredictable (Elder and Lees-Marshment 2021). Earlier poll leads eroded during the campaign, and as one post-election

1. Engage in a reconnection strategy with Canadian to rebuild the relationship between Trudeau and voters
2. Co-create a new way forward with Canadians
3. Refresh the team
4. Avoid calling an election without having devised a clear and well thought out branding strategy to avoid shifting approach mid-way

Fig. 2.3 Recommendations for practice

survey noted, "what appeared to be a relatively placid voter landscape was actually producing all sorts of movements" and there was "considerable churning throughout the election" (EKOS 2021). Given that the heart of political marketing lies in responding to the market, this will always make political branding very challenging, but even more necessary.

References

Primary Sources

Abacus (2021 August) 'What Canadians think about the federal deficit and the post-pandemic recovery' Conducted for the Broadbent Institute & the Professional Institute of the Public Service of Canada'
Abacus (2021 August 11) 'To reduce the deficit, Canadians want increased taxes on the wealthy and large corporations'
Abacus (2021 August 17) 'Affordability and the cost of living is the top issue for Canadians'
Abacus (2021 August 25) 'Canada's urban-rural divide'
Abacus (2021 August 26) 'What do Canadians think of the leaders?'
Abacus (2021 August 31) 'Into week three'
Abacus (2021 September 2) 'What issues are the parties owning and how has the campaign changed perceptions?'
Angus Reid (2021 August 30) 'Trudeau's troubles'
Angus Reid (2021 September 9) 'The issues'
EKOS (2021) Post-election survey
Ipsos (2021 September 15) 'Dead heat down the home stretch'
Ipsos (2021 4 September) 'Trudeau best choice for Prime Minister' press release
Liberal Ad (2021 August 15) ID: 1294482087616692
Liberal Ad (2021 August 16) ID: 545591143224531
Liberal Ad (2021 August 23) ID: 871558853764877
Liberal Ad (2021 August 24) ID: 531629014829735
Liberal Ad (2021 August 29) ID: 883102995897790
Liberal Ad (2021 August 31) ID: 2666584116974137

Liberal Ad (2021 September 1) ID: 997740591051334
Liberal Ad (2021 September 4) ID: 184472810421245
Liberal Ad (2021 September 7a) ID ID: 282953076599225
Liberal Ad (2021 September 7b) ID: 396324565185493
Liberal Ad (2021 September 7c) ID: 211490790960724
Liberal Ad (2021 September 8) ID: 172905798308146
Liberal Ad (2021 September 10) ID: 218028640347595
Liberal Ad (2021 September 11) ID: 1359427484451676
Liberal Ad (2021 September 14) 2021 ID: 694626228329821
Liberal Ad (2021 September 15a), ID: 256851062974606
Liberal Ad (2021 September 15b) ID: 1190947661416533
Liberal Ad (2021 September 15c) ID: 842828586411601
Liberal Ad (2021 September 15d) ID: 1028528174574532
Liberal Ad (2021 September 16a) ID: 346920310510660
Liberal Ad (2021 September 16b) ID: 560347985382545
Liberal Ad (2021 September 18a) ID: 4325700700825746
Liberal Ad (2021 September 18b) ID: 633914667593834
Liberal Media Release (2021 August 15) 'Team Trudeau launches campaign to move Canada forward—For everyone'
Liberal Media release (2021 August 16) 'New Liberal ad'
Liberal Media Release (2021 August 28) 'New Liberal ads'
Liberal Party (2021) Liberal Party Platform https://liberal.ca/our-platform/
Liberal Youtube (2021 August 15a) 'Relentless'
Liberal Youtube (2021 August 15b) 'Solidarité'
Liberal Youtube (2021 August 17) 'Pull Together'
Liberal Youtube (2021 August 25) 'A Home. For Everyone // Un chez-soi pour tous.'
Liberal Youtube (2021 August 29a) 'First Home'
Liberal Youtube (2021 August 29b) 'Bienvenue chez vous'
Liberal Youtube (2021 August 29c) 'Back to Normal'
Liberal Youtube (2021 August 29d) 'Retour à la normale'
Liberal Youtube (2021 September 5a) 'Take Back Canada'
Liberal Youtube (2021 September 5b) 'In his own words'
Liberal Youtube (2021 September 5c) 'The Record'
Liberal Youtube (2021 September 11) 'Avançons ensemble'
Liberal Youtube (2021 September 14) 'Stronger Gun Control'
Liberal Youtube (2021 September 17) 'Real Plan'
Liberal Youtube (2021 September 18a) 'Forward Now'
Liberal Youtube (2021 September 18b) 'Le moment d'avancer'
Liberal Youtube (2021 September 18c) 'Sammy's'
Liberal Youtube (2021 September 18d) 'Nafisa'
Liberal Youtube (2021 September 18e) 'Carlo'

Liberal Youtube (2021 September 18f) 'Patil'
Liberal Youtube (2021 September 18g) 'Home Grown'
Liberal Youtube (2021 September 20) 'Forward Now'
Trudeau, Justin (2021 August 15) Facebook Post
Trudeau, Justin (2021 August 16a) Facebook Post
Trudeau, Justin (2021 August 16b) Facebook Post
Trudeau, Justin (2021 August 17) Facebook Post
Trudeau, Justin (2021 August 25) Facebook Post
Trudeau, Justin (2021 August 30) Facebook Post
Trudeau, Justin (2021 September 12) Facebook Video
Trudeau, Justin (2021 September 18) Facebook Video
Trudeau, Justin (2021 September 19a) Facebook Post
Trudeau, Justin (2021 September 19b) Facebook Post
Trudeau, Justin (2021 September 19c) Facebook Post
Trudeau, Justin (2021 September 19d) 'Facebook Post'
Vote Compass Canada (2021) 'Jagmeet Singh seen as most competent and trustworthy leader: Vote Compass' CBC 9 September

Secondary Sources

Barberio, R.P. and B. M. Lowe (2006) 'Branding: Presidential politics and crafted political communications'. Paper for the 2006 Annual Meeting of the American Political Science Association

Downer, Lorann (2016) *Political branding strategies: Campaigning and governing in Australian politics.* Palgrave

Elder, E and J Lees-Marshment (ed.) (2021) *Political marketing and management in the 2020 New Zealand election.* Palgrave

Jalil, Ziena (2021) 'The COVID-19 election: How Labour turned a crisis into its biggest branding opportunity' in Elder, E and J Lees-Marshment (ed.) (2021) *Political marketing and management in the 2020 New Zealand election.* Palgrave, pp 35–45

Langmaid, R (2012). 'Co-creating the future'. In Jennifer Lees-Marshment (ed.) *Routledge handbook of political marketing.* New York: Routledge: 61–76

Lees-Marshment, J (2021) 'The new (old) Trudeau in 2019: The challenges and potential for branding Prime Ministers in Government' Chapter 2 in *Political marketing in 2019 Canadian federal election.* Palgrave, pp 11–26

Needham, C (2005) 'Brand leaders: Clinton, Blair and the limitations of the permanent campaign'. *Political Studies,* 53(2): 343–61

Smith, G (2009) 'Conceptualizing and testing brand personality in British politics'. *Journal of Political Marketing,* 8(3): 209–32

CHAPTER 3

Clowns to the Left of Me, Jokers to the Right: Branding Challenges in the 2021 Conservative Party Campaign

Jamie Gillies and Angela Wisniewski

Abstract The 2021 Conservative Party ran what should have been a successful campaign. A weakened prime minister, hobbled by the COVID-19 pandemic and the economic headwinds of inflation and uncertainty, was an easy target. Coupled with Jagmeet Singh's personal popularity and the relative strength of the Bloc Quebecois, the Tory campaign had a real opportunity to leapfrog the Liberals and win the most seats. Erin O'Toole tacked to the centre, even centre left, by releasing a 100-page plus platform and immediately running a policy wonkish campaign focused on issues the public cared about. They were hoping

J. Gillies (✉) · A. Wisniewski
Department of Journalism and Communications, St. Thomas University, Fredericton, NB, Canada
e-mail: jgillies@stu.ca

A. Wisniewski
e-mail: awisn@stu.ca

© The Author(s), under exclusive license to Springer Nature Switzerland AG 2023
J. Gillies et al. (eds.), *Political Marketing in the 2021 Canadian Federal Election*, Palgrave Studies in Political Marketing and Management,
https://doi.org/10.1007/978-3-031-34404-6_3

to mimic the surprise provincial victory by the Tim Houston-led Progressive Conservatives in Nova Scotia in the first week of the campaign. Alas, it was not to last as the softening of the Conservative brand did not break through. Familiar narratives, like gun control and sheep-in-wolf's-clothing attacks, hammered O'Toole in the middle of the campaign and despite presenting a bigger tent image of the party, the Conservatives wound up exactly where they were with Andrew Scheer two years earlier. This chapter considers the bind that the Conservative Party marketing and branding strategists found themselves in appeal to the populist right and alienate moderate voters who are key to a Tory majority government, tack to the centre and alienate the grassroots right, with their focus on everything from vaccination mandates to less government intervention to immigration. The brand is at odds with the political market it hopes to win. It contrasts the O'Toole campaign in 2021 with the Scheer campaign in 2019 and looks at whether the anti-Justin Trudeau message that had become the mantra of the party through three elections simply did not resonate beyond the base.

Keywords Erin O'Toole · Pierre Poilievre · Conservative Party of Canada · Rebranding · Campaign

Introduction

The 2019 federal election was a big disappointment for the Conservative Party of Canada (CPC). Justin Trudeau's brand and image had suffered a remarkable setback in 2018 as the SNC Lavalin scandal broke and with the ouster of Jody Wilson-Raybould as Attorney General of Canada (Lees-Marshment 2019). Andrew Scheer, who was marketed as a Stephen Harper-lite leader, offered a bigger tent strategy in the hopes of winning back many of the suburban ridings lost to Trudeau and the Liberals in 2015 (Boutilier 2018). Scheer's campaign, despite moments in which he rose to the occasion such as challenging People's Party leader Maxime Bernier in leadership debates, was lackluster and it failed to offer a key vision in how to differentiate itself from the Liberals (Radwanski 2019). The 2019 campaign was simply anti-Trudeau and it failed to deliver the most seats. It did knock the Liberals down to a minority government but the knives were out on election night. Scheer would resign as leader in 2020 amidst caucus and party criticisms of his leadership.

The 2019 election should have been a warning sign to the CPC. The Trudeau brand was simply stronger than the anti-Trudeau brand, despite Conservatives' best efforts to go negative on and continue to personally attack Trudeau. The CPC also conducted a post-mortem process of the 2019 election campaign and what went wrong (Simpson 2019). It found that voters still did not trust the Conservative brand and still had hostility to the Stephen Harper years (Coletto et al. 2019).

Consequently, the 2020 Conservative leadership race presented the CPC with an opportunity in terms of a rebranding and new avenues to target voters in the lead up to the next election. The challenge was that, despite getting more votes than a weakened Liberal Party in the 2019 election, the CPC needed to win in three major Canadian metropolitan areas: Toronto, Montreal and Vancouver. Concentrated vote support in Alberta, Saskatchewan and rural British Columbia and Manitoba did not give the party the conditions to win a general election. They failed to win more than a handful of ridings east of Ontario and they had one of the worst vote distributions in Canadian history. The Liberals, meanwhile, had near-perfect vote distribution, when close races in most competitive Ontario and suburban ridings. The CPC still had a marketing problem where most of the public lived. The Stephen Harper years continued to be an albatross in 2019 and Scheer's soccer Dad version of Harper did not win over voters in the places the CPC needed to win (Lewsen 2019).

There were other problems for the CPC as well. Maxime Bernier, Scheer's closest rival for the leadership to take over from Harper, had left the party and formed the People's Party of Canada. Capitalizing on populist and extremist rhetoric and alt-right dissatisfaction with right of centre parties, Bernier set out to re-establish a populist movement that had been absorbed when the Reform Party/Alliance has been absorbed into the unite the right CPC. But where the Reform/Alliance had been grounded in Preston Manning's ideology of a Western Canadian centrality to break the Laurentian Consensus of Toronto to Montreal domination of Canadian politics, Bernier's People's Party is a weird mix of libertarianism, Christian nationalism and the alt-right extremism opposed to immigration. Andrew Scheer was able to beat back Bernier's right-wing overtures in the 2019 election, painting him as an opportunistic hypocrite and condemning the People's Party as representing the worst instincts in people. Bernier's support was around 1% in the 2019 election and did not lead to much vote-splitting on the right in ridings where it would have made a difference (Berthiaume 2019).

Between 2019 and the 2021 election, however, the pandemic and the government's response including masking, distancing and vaccination mandates, gave Bernier and the People's Party a set of policy issues around which to rally. This presented the CPC with a problem. Now they were being squeezed more from the right. So the 2020 CPC leadership race then became a test of a new brand and marketing strategy based on the 2019 election audit and what went wrong. The CPC needed to reach new voters and re-capture at least some of the middle from Liberals. A 5–10% shift with enough voters and their vote concentration and distribution would look a lot more like the Liberals as well.

This certainly factored into the three campaigns that would ultimately lead the 2020 CPC leadership race. Peter MacKay, representing the old-guard Progressive Conservative wing, claimed the 2019 election should have been an easy win and that it was like "scoring an own goal." Leslyn Lewis, representing the more social conservative faction, ran in an attempt to reframe the party along more traditional family values and social issues lines like abortion. Erin O'Toole, as a former Canadian Forces captain and lawyer, was a compromise candidate, splitting the difference between MacKay and Lewis. He ran to the right in the leadership contest, and with the rank choice voting system, was able to perform better with supporters of more conservative candidates like Lewis. O'Toole eventually prevailed in the third round of voting. He pitched himself as a "true blue conservative," which allowed him to pivot to the right of MacKay (Tasker 2020).

In some ways, O'Toole's 2020 leadership campaign is indicative of many of the challenges right of centre parties are facing. This is part of a larger branding and marketing problem that has existed since the rise of both Boris Johnson and Donald Trump. These party coalitions are fragmented and polarized along different dividing lines. Whereas the traditional coalitions of social conservatives, fiscal conservatives and military hawks that formed the backbone of most conservative party support, these new and ascendant groups did not fit into those categories. In its most reductive, this meant new branding and marketing opportunities for conservative parties to reach out to newly activated voters. But it also can come with a tremendous cost if old and enduring brands are collapsed to allow for right-wing populist appeals. For Erin O'Toole, it represented a problem for a middle of the road leader. Do you market and brand the campaign to the base? Or do you reach out to unaffiliated and middle of the road voters in an attempt to expand the brand? A classic, clowns to the left of me, jokers to the right scenario.

Haphazard Brand Restructuring

For the CPC coming out of the 2019 election, there were some serious marketing challenges. Hamish Marshall, who had been the party's pollster in the Stephen Harper and had led Scheer's campaign team, was a seasoned veteran inheriting a tried and tested conservative brand (Ryckewaert 2019). Justin Trudeau's image and trust in the Liberal government had fallen dramatically in the lead up to the 2019 election. There was every belief within CPC circles that they had a winnable strategy that year. It did not work that way. In 2019, the party conducted both a post-mortem of Scheer's leadership and on the 2019 campaign. It demonstrated that the party, despite Trudeau's unpopularity, could not win with just an anti-Trudeau message (Wherry 2019). It also showed that the brand was not at all popular in most of Quebec and Atlantic Canada, remained cool in the Toronto suburbs and, despite increased anger about Trudeau between Kamloops, B.C. and Winnipeg, Manitoba, this translated into very few additional seats in 2019.

Scheer's attempt to stay on as leader further drove a division between the PC base and the Prairie base, with MacKay floated as a replacement almost from day one. The problems also stemmed from residuals leftover from the Stephen Harper era (Marland 2016). The Liberals continued to do an effective job as the anti-Stephen Harper brand. Harper and his leadership had proved stubbornly unpopular in Canada, even after Scheer took over. The public still equated Harper with poor leadership and that allowed the Liberals to use the Harper boogeyman in the 2019 election. In many respects, it was more durable than the anti-Trudeau branding of the CPC.

In retrospect, Erin O'Toole faced internal party headwinds from the moment he won the leadership race. The right-wing base and some strategists believed that O'Toole was not a true blue conservative. O'Toole thought triangulation of the brand could build a government in waiting and could defeat Trudeau. That schism, while certainly not a civil war, played a part in how O'Toole shifted the CPC brand in 2021 from the Harper years to an election platform that tried to be all things to all people.

In some ways, the 2021 election came at a bad time for the CPC. Trudeau again tried to time an election in the hopes of regaining a majority government. Favourable polling showed the Liberals with about a five-point lead nationally in the lead up to the writ being dropped (Kilpatrick 2021). The CPC, however, had to pitch to voters in the middle of a pandemic. It was not an election to double down on a more conservative economic or social message since the country was still reeling from COVID-19. So the odd timing made the branding and marketing of the O'Toole brand potentially a one-off unless it was successful.

Prior to the election, the CPC attempted to create a positive image of O'Toole. Unlike Harper and Scheer, O'Toole was more personable and he genuinely liked the campaign trail. He also had a compelling personal story, served honourably in the military and made the pre-writ campaign a focus on his personable attributes in contrast to Trudeau. O'Toole developed a folksy by centrist message, talking at campaign events as the proud son of a union-supporting mother. He also eschewed any social conservative appeals, marching in pride parades and marketing the CPC as a big tent party for every Canadian. He also focused the economic message not on tax cuts or traditional conservative talking points but on taking inequality seriously.

This had been part of the strategy since O'Toole won the leadership contest. Fred DeLorey became the CPC campaign manager, after leading O'Toole's victory in 2020. The campaign team also were a group of O'Toole insiders and stalwarts from the successful 2011 Harper campaign team including deputy national campaign manager Laura Kurkimaki and Chief Strategist Dan Robertson. Robertson ran advertising in the successful 2011 election for the CPC (Ryckewaert 2021).

When the writ was dropped, O'Toole immediately released his CPC election platform entitled *Secure The Future*. This document is one of the most fascinating rebranding attempts in recent Canadian political campaigns. Eschewing the party's own convention votes by party rank and file, including but not limited to, iffy support for abortion access and a vote that climate change was not caused by humans, O'Toole team crafted an almost left-of-centre policy platform and positive Liberal Party-lite campaign messaging. This was in stark contrast to Scheer's single-issue anti-Trudeau messaging. O'Toole even made the discussion of Trudeau an afterthought, focusing instead on pocket book issues, affordability, inequality and openness. The Secure The Future document and campaign promises were arguably to the left of the U.S. Democratic Party's entire agenda. It was the rare Canadian election where the three major parties and the vast majority of the political spectrum were to the left of the entire U.S. system.

For observers, it felt odd to see the two largest parties almost in agreement on every major social and economic issues. While some called it opportunistic, for the first two weeks of the 2021 election campaign, it seemed to work. Trudeau's lead in the polls evaporated and O'Toole started to lead in the polls. In some respects, this was as effective a rebranding as could have been achieved in such a short time. O'Toole was not from the Harper/Scheer wing of the party, but he also was not old school Joe Clark/Peter MacKay Progressive Conservative either. He fits within the provincial Progressive Conservative Ontario coalition of Doug Ford and Christine Elliott. His conservatism was a mix of military straight-lacedness and a broad middle-class economic conservatism within the suburban striver demographic. On paper, O'Toole was as good a candidate the CPC could have come with for a leader in going after the 75 or so suburban ridings they needed to win. O'Toole also came across as the best leader versus Trudeau. He was able to concentrate on selling himself in the campaign as opposed to pure negative partisanship messaging. By the end of the second week, the Liberals must have realized their election call was a disaster.

O'Toole was also gifted a campaign strategy literally on the first day of the election. Nova Scotia's Liberal Party had called an election, and like the Trudeau Liberals, seemed to have about a five-point lead in the polls (Wentzell 2021). But the Nova Scotia Progressive Conservatives, under leader Tim Houston, focused entirely on issues like access to health care. They toned down any talk of social conservatism or cutting services and focused on flaws in policy leadership during the pandemic. The Nova Scotia PCs won a majority government. O'Toole's team likely saw a parallel with Houston's election win. The public was craving no-nonsense solutions to policy challenges.

It made sense that O'Toole spent the bulk of his time early on in the campaign in the Greater Toronto Area. A native of Bowmanville, Ontario, just outside of Oshawa, at the eastern edge of the GTA, O'Toole pitched the CPC as the suburban big tent alternative to the downtown elite Liberals. Part of that brand appeal was his stump speech. O'Toole characterized himself as a pro-choice LGBTQ+ ally who grew up in a union household. These were not characteristic of Tory leaders in the past. Liberal strategist David Herle saw this as a truly Progressive Conservative election campaign, which had not been attempted since the years of Joe Clark's leadership in the 1990s and 2000s (Chase and Bailey 2021).

The other innovation that gave O'Toole an early boost was DeLorey's and Robertson's strategy to build a virtual studio at the Westin Hotel in downtown Ottawa. This allowed O'Toole to conduct multiple virtual campaign events and cover parts of the country more rapidly. It also allowed the O'Toole brand to be reinforced with campaign workers and different candidates and provide rapid response to Liberal and other party attacks, as well as professional media events that networks could run (Thibedeau 2021).

Brand Limitations

With Justin Trudeau, his brand overtook the Liberal Party brand very early. It became about his style of leadership. But with Scheer and O'Toole, overcoming the baked-in Harper/CPC brand was considerably more difficult. Part of it is that the CPC base is not like O'Toole. He may have been middle of the road as a leadership candidate, a compromise between prairie conservatives and suburban conservatives but with the leftward shift for the campaign, most Tory voters would have been further right than the platform. Almost immediately, there were accusations that O'Toole's brand did not fit with the core principles of the party. But there were others who recognized that the rebranding was designed to appeal specifically to middle of the road voters in vote-rich places like the suburban GTA.

At the halfway point of the campaign, the O'Toole brand restructuring no longer resonated. The media and the Liberals seized on O'Toole's position on gun control. It had not been a major factor in the campaign thus far. Trudeau was still trying to justify the election amidst the pandemic and that the fall of Afghanistan to the Taliban became the political news focus overshadowing stories on the hustings (MacCharles and Levitz 2021). But with gun control, O'Toole's campaign simply let this unforced error fester as O'Toole promised one thing at one event, then flipped and promised something else the next day. The brand restructure, around a personable centrist, started to lose momentum,

Trudeau then received a polling bump gift when protestors started heckling and throwing gravel at him at a Bolton, Ontario campaign stop towards the end of August 2021. With only a couple weeks left in the election, it was revealed that some of those protestors in the crowd were Conservative party campaign workers. It went from a protest to violence against the prime minister and the CPC was left with a broken brand narrative.

O'Toole never recovered and on Election Day, despite leading in the polls through the early part of the campaign, he failed to get any more seats than his predecessor Andrew Scheer. O'Toole discovered, like Scheer, that negative brand association with the CPC outweighed the brand restructure around him. O'Toole, like 2012 U.S. presidential candidate Mitt Romney, tried to lift the party brand. And despite both of them having campaign moments that allowed them to surge, ultimately the brand legacies would hurt their momentum and end in defeat. For O'Toole, it was an "old wine in a new bottle" problem. Voters were willing to give him a chance but the moment the brand restructure started to emulate the old Harper brand, with Harper-style policies, the gig was up. It also showed the limitations of falling back on the CPC anti-Trudeau brand. Three elections, three losses and Trudeau's image and brand, while reduced on stature, still endured. Further, the creeping alt-right and far-right insurrectionist violence became a narrative in the campaign and even O'Toole, who shifted as far as a centre-right candidate could from this, was undone by careless optics and control at Trudeau events. It was a rebrand that broke halfway through the campaign.

The O'Toole Rebrand Fallout

While the 2021 CPC campaign was interesting in terms of the horse race dynamics interacting with what O'Toole and his campaign team were trying to do with a party and leader rebranding, the fallout from O'Toole's election loss is more important to this election cycle narrative. Between September 2021 and March 2022, the CPC's political brand shifted dramatically as O'Toole was ousted from leadership amidst the trucker convoy protests that exploded into the Canadian political mainstream.

Further, Pierre Poilievre, who helped orchestrate O'Toole's downfall with the caucus revolt vote, and became the front-runner for leadership in 2022, saw his opportunity to kill the old CPC brand. The trucker protests gave Poilievre his populist firebrand pivot and allowed him to shore up the base of the party easily.

O'Toole was the perfect foil for this. He represented the old wing of the party that was not in ascendancy. The energy was with people opposing Trudeau in the streets and Poilievre's calculation was that these groups needed a leader, otherwise that vote would go to Maxime Bernier and the populist People's Party. O'Toole's brand then represented everything Poilievre did not want: it merged the buttoned-down Harper consensus image with a progressive conservative rebranding. Poilievre wanted the Harper base merged with an increasingly disaffected group of voters that Poilievre feels can grow the party and defeat Trudeau and the Liberals.

Far tamer than American elections, Canada has nonetheless had a nativist populist streak for decades. But rarely have those elements been central to power in Ottawa. Poilievre represents a completely new conservative brand that the Canadian political scene has never really seen. The moments of populist insurgency on the right in Canada have come at the expense of political unification. The Reform Party and Canadian Alliance split the vote with the Progressive Conservatives and left them out of power for four consecutive elections. Prior to that, John Diefenbaker's populism was a one and done phenomenon as haphazard policy decisions and generational mistakes like cancelling Canada's aerospace industry left the party out of power for almost twenty years.

The 2022 trucker protests demonstrated the seething underbelly of Canadian politics (Gillies et al. 2023). The protests emerged in a pattern that typifies a "new blueprint of grassroots political action" (Lalancette and Raynauld 2020), whereby Canadian movements adopt decentralized, fluid and fragmented patterns of mobilizing, communicating and organizing. The trucker movement initially coalesced around objections to federal vaccine mandates, but quickly fragmented to include distinct subgroup agendas (including anti-Trudeau groups and extremist groups), as well as individual members who took part in the movement as a forum for expressing their unique personal narratives and concerns (Gillies et al. 2023). Poilievre tapped into the fragmented and fluid characteristics of the movement, publicly applauding protestors for carrying a wide range of problems and concerns to Ottawa. For instance, Poilievre praised the protest as encompassing a wide array of personal concerns: "[T]he 60-year-old small businessman who has spent his entire adult life building up an enterprise and watching it wiped out … the depressed 14-year-old who's been locked out of school…[and]…the families that can't take it anymore". (Poilievre quoted in Wherry 2022).

Poilievre played to the populist spirit animating the trucker protests with messages like his #FreedomOverFear, which depicted federal decision-makers of conspiratorially using the pandemic as an opportunity to take away personal freedoms (Wherry 2022). This messaging evokes populist styles of thinking that gained traction during the first years of the pandemic, including distrust of political, social and scientific elites believed to be using the pandemic to extend political control; expressions of outrage at a purported "betrayal" of everyday, upright, people; and intense and reductive moral judgements (Eberl et al 2021; Brubaker 2021). Poilievre has branded himself as a champion of personal freedoms for Canadians, and the emergence of a populist protest movement gave him the opportunity to reinforce a key element of his personal brand (Proudfoot 2022).

Months after the trucker protests, Poilievre's commitment to the trucker convoy has become a source of speculation. Journalists have noted that Poilievre has rarely come to the defense of protest organizers during the Public Order Emergency Commission (Kopecky 2022). While some believe that Poilievre may have "burnt his hands" by showing enthusiastic support for a broadly unpopular movement, others note that he continues to rely on populist messaging, including critiques of institutions like the World Economic Forum and cultivating an image that he understands the plight of the everyday working Canadians (Kopecky 2022; The Economist 2022).

Bernier's formation of the People's Party was handled deftly by Scheer in the 2019 election campaign as it failed to cost the CPC a split of the right but O'Toole completely left Bernier to his own devices. The vaccination and masking mandates gave the far right a huge opening to give Bernier a platform in the 2021 election campaign. This time, Bernier and the PPC took almost 5% of the vote and over 840,000 votes. That vote split terrified the CPC who were lucky to hold the 119 seats they had won previously. Had O'Toole won, Canada likely would have avoided an extended conversation about the populist right in the mainstream of Canadian politics. But he did not win and the CPC brand that had been built since the Harper unite the right movement was broken.

For O'Toole, he was quickly shown the door, with grassroots leaders and CPC MPs alike deriding the election strategy to move to the middle and centre left in order to appeal to the suburbs. Voters apparently saw right through it: Liberal-light is still worse than Liberal. O'Toole, instead of being lauded as a political moderate with policy ideas in tune with the Canadian public, was lambasted as a phony by his own party for selling out its values.

Branding Populism and Extremism

The O'Toole election failure may have long-term branding consequences for parties going forward. The Liberals, NDP and CPC had all largely kept right-wing and left-wing populist extremism at bay, using both internal safety valves within parties and in their branding and marketing and appeals to voters. With Poilievre's ascendancy to the CPC, especially with a stronger populist appeal, the CPC will be forced to go after these voters. That brings those voices inside the tent, something both O'Toole and Scheer rejected either on principle or for political reasons. The bigger concern is that it increases the toxification of the political discourse and leads to an increase in the radicalization of political messaging (Brewster 2023).

The CPC brand shift under Poilievre has the potential of course to defeat Trudeau and the Liberals. It also has the potential of a high-risk, low-reward eventuality, in that Poilievre may have missed his moment in harnessing populism. Mandates are over and Canada is shifting to pandemic mitigation and a post-pandemic environment so unifying these voices of the right may become more difficult.

O'Toole's rebranding attempts likely are the last vestige of the old Progressive Conservative brand. Unique to western democracies, the Progressive Conservatives are a somewhat unique alliance of social progressives who favour conservative economic ad governing principles. That wing of the newer CPC had always had a voice in decisions and lead the right of centre in Canada from 1942 until the "unite the right" movements of the 2000s. But Jean Charest's failure to mount a serious challenge to Poilievre and his subsequent gutting of that wing of the party from positions of power since 2022 seems to be an end of the kind of party positioning in going after the "soft" Liberal vote. That party polarization that Poilievre, and Harper before him, desires likely means that the CPC cannot brand and market in the same way. It becomes difficult to manage a campaign when traditionally, all of the parties target the middle of the road voter. For Poilievre, he probably has to target the far right and create a groundswell of voters who often are excluded from the mainstream process or simply have not voted in the past. This makes for some strange bedfellows in Canadian politics.

It also likely means that the branding of parties and the marketing of leaders will hew towards a far more American-style emotive communications, pitting values against each other, as opposed to policy and character differences.

REFERENCES

Berthiaume, Lee. 2019. "Upstart People's Party had little impact on election results: Analysis." *CTV News*, October 23, 2019, https://www.ctvnews.ca/politics/federal-election-2019/upstart-people-s-party-had-little-impact-on-election-results-analysis-1.4652140

Boutilier, Alex. 2018. "Key question for conservatives: Who's inside the Big Blue Tent?" *Toronto Star*, August 26, 2018, https://www.thestar.com/news/canada/analysis/2018/08/26/key-question-for-conservatives-whos-inside-the-big-blue-tent.html

Brewster, Murray. 2023. "Canada is picking up the political radicalization bug from the U.S., new report warns." *CBC News*, January 3, 2023, https://www.cbc.ca/news/politics/canada-political-polarization-maga-trudeau-poilievre-russia-1.6702856

Brubaker, Rogers. 2021. "Paradoxes of populism during the pandemic." *Thesis Eleven, 164*(1) 73–87.

Chase, Steven and Ian Bailey. 2021. "Conservative leader Erin O'Toole's ideology shift was not enough to surpass Liberals." *Globe & Mail*, September 21, 2021, https://www.theglobeandmail.com/politics/article-conservative-leader-erin-otooles-ideology-shift-was-not-enough-to/

Coletto, David, Harrison, Kate and Dennis Matthews. 2019. "The state of the Conservative Party brand at the end of 2019." *Abacus Data*, https://abacusdata.ca/conservative-party-brand-canada-abacus-data-branding/

Eberl, Jakob-Moritz, Huber, Robert A. & Esther Greussing. 2021. "From populism to the 'plandemic': Why populists believe in Covid-19 conspiracies." *Journal of Elections, Public Opinion and Parties, 31*(1), 272–284.

The Economist, "Canada's Trump" is politer than the real thing. *The Economist*, June 11, 2022, https://www.economist.com/the-americas/2022/06/09/canadas-trump-is-politer-than-the-real-thing

Gillies, Jamie, Vincent Raynauld and Angela Wisniewski. 2023. "Canada is no exception: Freedom convoy 2022 and identity-driven political protest." *American Behavioral Scientist (Forthcoming 2023).*

Kilpatrick, Sean. 2021. "Liberals take five-point lead in poll as Canada's 2021 federal election campaign begins." *Globe & Mail*, August 17, 2021, https://www.theglobeandmail.com/politics/article-liberals-take-five-point-lead-in-poll-as-federal-election-campaign/

Kopecky, Arno. 2022. 'Freedom Convoy' protest ignited, Canada boiled over and Poilievre's Conservatives burnt their hands. *Canada's National Observer*, December 7 2022, https://www.nationalobserver.com/2022/12/07/opinion/freedom-convoy-protest-canada-poilievre-conservatives

Lalancette, Mireille and Vincent Raynauld. 2020. Online mobilization: Tweeting truth to power in an era of revised patterns of mobilization in Canada. In Tamara Small & Harold Jansen (Eds). *Digital politics in Canada: Promises and realities*, (pp. 223–244). Toronto: University of Toronto Press.

Lees-Marshment, Jennifer. 2019. "The new (Old) Trudeau in 2019: The challenges and potential for branding Prime Ministers in government." In *Political marketing in the 2019 Canadian Election*. Eds. Jamie Gillies, Vincent Raynauld and André Turcotte. London: Palgrave.

Lewsen, Simon. 2019. "The man who could beat Justin Trudeau." *The Atlantic*, October 17, 2019, https://www.theatlantic.com/international/archive/2019/10/andrew-scheer-canada-politics-election/600046/

MacCharles, Tonda and Stephanie Levitz. 2021. "Guns, gravel and old-fashioned hustle: The inside story of how Justin Trudeau stopped Erin O'Toole's momentum and held on to power." *Toronto Star*, September 22, 2021, https://www.thestar.com/politics/federal-election/2021/09/22/guns-gravel-and-old-fashioned-hustle-the-inside-story-of-how-justin-trudeau-stopped-erin-otooles-momentum-and-held-on-to-power.html

Marland, Alex. 2016. *Brand command: Canadian politics and democracy in the age of message control*. Vancouver: UBC Press.

Proudfoot, Shannon. 2022. Why is Pierre Poilievre so angry? He's smart, savvy and he's steering a new brand of Canadian conservatism. How Pierre Poilievre became the champion of the Anti-Trudeau mob. *Maclean's*, March 10, 2022, https://www.macleans.ca/longforms/why-is-pierre-poilievre-so-angry/

Radwanski, Adam. 2019. "Federal election 2019: The vote was Scheer's to win, but he failed to expand support beyond the Conservative base." *Globe & Mail*, October 22, 2019, https://www.theglobeandmail.com/canada/article-federal-election-2019-the-vote-was-scheers-to-win-but-he-failed-to/

Ryckewaert, Laura. 2019. "Tried and tested team behind Conservative Party's bid to return to government." *The Hill Times*, September 16, 2019, https://www.hilltimes.com/2019/09/16/tried-and-tested-team-behind-conservative-partys-bid-to-return-to-government/214169.

Ryckewaert, Laura. 2021. "O'Toole backed by fresh but familiar team for digital-heavy 2021 Conservative campaign." *The Hill Times*, September 1, 2021, https://www.hilltimes.com/story/2021/09/01/otoole-backed-by-fresh-but-familiar-team-for-digital-heavy-2021-conservative-campaign/229578/

Simpson, Katie. 2019. "Conservatives reviewing election near-miss as Andrew Scheer makes pitch to stay on as leader." *CBC News*, October 23,

2019, https://www.cbc.ca/news/politics/andrew-scheer-conservative-2019-federal-election-1.5332912

Tasker, John Paul. 2020. "Erin O'Toole launches Conservative leadership bid, promises to be the 'true blue' candidate." *CBC News*, January 27, 2020, https://www.cbc.ca/news/politics/erin-otoole-conservative-leadership-bid-1.5441642

Thibedeau, Hannah. 2021. "Conservatives say their 'virtual' campaign strategy is paying off already." *CBC News*, August 27, 2021, https://www.cbc.ca/news/politics/otoole-conservative-election-virtual-campaign-town-hall-pandemic-1.6154822

Wentzell, Stephen. 2021. "New poll finds N.S. Liberals leading in support." *Halifax CityNews*, August 5, 2021, https://halifax.citynews.ca/local-news/new-poll-finds-ns-liberals-leading-in-support-4194698

Wherry, Aaron. 2019. "Andrew Scheer doesn't seem to be quite done fighting the election yet." *CBC News*, December 6, 2019, https://www.cbc.ca/news/politics/andrew-scheer-justin-trudeau-2019-election-1.5387126

Wherry, Aaron. 2022. Conservatives hitch their wagon to the convoy protest without knowing where it's going. *CBC News*, February. 1, 2022, https://www.cbc.ca/news/politics/poilievre-conservative-otoole-convoy-vaccine-mandate-1.6335286

CHAPTER 4

The Hyper–Masculine Campaign: Party Leader Brand Image, Heteronormativity and the 2021 Canadian Federal Election

Mireille Lalancette and Vincent Raynauld

Abstract This chapter takes an interest in Canadian party leaders' mobilization of hypermasculine political communication and marketing strategies during the 2021 federal election. Building on a visual and textual content analysis of Instagram posts and digital ads shared by

---

Manuscript to be submitted for the edited collection titled "Political Marketing in the 2021 Canadian Federal Elections" edited by Jamie Gillies, Vincent Raynauld and André Turcotte.

A version of this chapter was presented at the 2022 Northeastern Political Science Association Annual Conference in Boston, Massachusetts. The paper was awarded the NPSA's Identity Politics Best Paper Award for 2022.

M. Lalancette (✉)
Départment de Lettres et Communication Sociale, Université du Québec à Trois-Rivières, Trois-Rivières, QC, Canada
e-mail: mireille.lalancette@uqtr.ca

© The Author(s), under exclusive license to Springer Nature Switzerland AG 2023
J. Gillies et al. (eds.), *Political Marketing in the 2021 Canadian Federal Election*, Palgrave Studies in Political Marketing and Management, https://doi.org/10.1007/978-3-031-34404-6_4

leaders of all major federal parties, this paper shows how leadership was framed as in a highly contested, personalized and masculine electoral race. Leaders used image-making and messaging techniques leveraging metaphors, images and frames building on and emphasizing their masculine traits. Most notably, Conservative Party of Canada's (CPC) Erin O'Toole was pictured in a tight t-shirt on the frontpage of the CPC electoral program. He was also defined as "the man with the plan". Other leaders used similar strategies throughout the campaign. This paper fills gaps in the academic literature in Canada as it unpacks the role of gender—most specifically masculinity—in party dynamics and identity political marketing in Canada. This chapter also makes a methodological contribution by developing a coding approach identifying direct and indirect appeals to masculinity in electoral political marketing strategies. Direct appeals include the highlighting of masculinity in political leadership, while indirect ones include discussions of political and policy issues related to elements of masculinity (e.g., strength, power, assertiveness). While some research has been done on identity-based uses of social media in political campaigns, this paper spotlights this dynamic in digital political communication and marketing, which has been under-researched. More broadly, it offers a timely look at the dynamics of digital political marketing during election campaigns.

Keywords Political communication · Political campaigning · Canadian Politics · Political marketing · Gender · Masculinity · Identity politics

Overview

When Canadian Prime Minister Justin Trudeau—accompanied by members of his family—made his way to Rideau Hall to meet with governor general Mary Simon and ask for the dissolution of the 43rd Parliament on August 14, 2021, he triggered a snap election that would stand out from previous campaigns in several ways. For example, Canada

---

V. Raynauld
Department of Communication Studies, Emerson College, Boston, MA, USA
e-mail: vincent_raynauld@emerson.edu

was in the midst of the COVID-19 global pandemic, which required the implementation and enforcement of strict, and in many cases disruptive, public health measures limiting the spread of the SARS-CoV-2 virus. These measures upended several facets of Canadians' daily life. For example, students at all education levels were forced to stay home and adapt to—in many cases—unfamiliar online pedagogical approaches on short notice (Marshall, Roache et al. 2020; Metcalfe 2021). Patterns of family and social life were also altered severely due to "social isolation, travel bans, border closures" and limitations on the size and timing of in-person gatherings (Faulkner, Rhodes et al. 2020). Additionally, the COVID-19 mitigation efforts took a toll on Canadians' well-being, many of whom reported high levels of stress and anxiety due to "situations derived from the COVID-19 lockdown" (Canzi and Danioni 2021: 1304). Finally, and of particular interest for this edited collection, the COVID-19 health emergency required politicians across party lines to rethink and adjust the format of their campaigning activities during the 2021 Canadian federal elections in order to respect COVID-19 restrictions and insure the safety of the public (e.g. Bryden 2021; Elections Canada 2021). Among them include Conservative Party of Canada (CPC) leader Erin O'Toole who pre-recorded announcements and other messages in a television studio and shared them through his and his party's social media channels (see Fig. 4.1) (Austen 2021).

Second, the Canadian economy was in a state of "medically induced coma" caused by the aforementioned COVID-19 public health restrictions (Lemieux, Milligan et al. 2020: 555). They contributed to slowing or shutting down many sectors of economic activity and modifying labour market practices (e.g., work-from-home models, reimagining of the production and delivery of goods and services) (Fuller and Qian: 2021; Lemieux, Milligan et al. 2020). A 2021 Statistics Canada survey also revealed that many Canadians lost their jobs, worked less paid hours and struggled to fulfil "basic household financial" obligations, especially among minority and marginalized segments of the Canadian society (Statistics Canada 2021). It should be noted that the late spring and summer months preceding the dropping of the writ were marked by local, provincial and federal governments easing progressively some COVID-19 restrictions and taking steps to and reinvigorate the economy (Fuller and Qian: 2021; Lawson, Nathans et al. 2022).

Lastly, the state of public health and the economy in Canada reshaped many aspects of voters' political attitudes, interests and objectives ahead

Fig. 4.1 Screenshot of an Instagram post on Erin O'Toole's personal account featuring an announcement from CPC campaign studios shared during the campaign

of the elections. From a policy perspective, as Canada emerged from the more acute phases of the COVID-19 pandemic during the summer months of 2021, a July 2021 CTV News/Nanos poll (2021) showed that the economy, the environment and the deficit topped Canadian voters' policy priorities and were likely to shape their decision on Election Day (see also: Kishchuk 2021). Among the economic issues of particular public interest were the cost of living, housing and taxes (Kishchuk 2021). Only 10% of respondents considered the COVID-19 pandemic to be the main policy matter likely to influence their choice on Election Day (CTV News/Nanos 2021). From a more political perspective, an August 2021 Leger survey revealed that the Liberal Party of Canada (LPC) was leading in the voting intentions—closely followed by the CPC—and was perceived to be the "most competent party for post-pandemic recovery". LPC's Justin Trudeau was also seen as the party "leader who would make the best prime minister" (Leger 2021b). However, other surveys indicated that Trudeau's Liberals faced political headwinds. For example, a

2021 Léger poll (2021a) indicated that a majority of respondents (52%) reported being dissatisfied with the performance of their government. In fact, a mid-August 2021 Abacus Data poll indicated that only 41% of respondents believed Canada was headed in the right direction. Furthermore, Trudeau was perceived negatively by 44% of respondents compared to 41% for CPC leader Erin O'Toole and 24% for New Democratic Party (NDP) leader Jagmeet Singh (Anderson and Coletto 2021). Finally, an August 2021 Mainstreet Research poll (2021) found that 65% of Canadians questioned the timing of the elections, with the highest level of disapproval among Canadians aged 65 or over and undecided voters.

As the dropping of the writ coincided with a unique moment of political, social and economic uncertainty and recovery in Canada, this book chapter zeroes in on how major-party leaders crafted electioneering strategies tailored to the aforementioned dynamics to appeal to, connect with and secure the support of voters. While LPC's Justin Trudeau (e.g., Marland 2018; Musial and Mintz 2021; Lalancette and Raynauld 2020) and, to a much lesser degree, NDP's Jagmeet Singh's (e.g., Bouchard 2022; McLean 2021) political communication and marketing tactics have received some scholarly attention, few researchers have taken interest in CPC leader Erin O'Toole's political image-making and voter appeal strategies.

CPC's O'Toole—who served as CPC leader until February 2022 when he resigned following his loss of a secret-ballot confidence vote (Aiello 2022)—is a case study of particular interest. First, polls conducted before and throughout the electoral campaign showed that the CPC was the LPC's most serious competitor in a context of crisis and widespread desire for political change among Canadian voters (e.g., CBC News 2021; Leger 2021a, b; Mainstreet Research 2021). Second, as O'Toole was elected CPC leader in late August 2020, he was relatively unknown on the national political stage. This gave him the opportunity to roll out and manage his public brand image in ways of positioning himself and the CPC policy offerings strategically in a crowded and somewhat fragmented electoral arena (Bolton 2022). While the incumbency advantage is well documented in the scholarly literature (e.g., Carson, Sievert et al. 2020; da Vinha and Ernst 2018; Sevi 2022), most other major-party leaders— who were well-known among the Canadian electorate—had limited time and flexibility to tweak their public image and narrative in a context of crisis, uncertainty and recovery (Bolton 2022). In the context of this paper, a crisis is defined as an "uncertain, complex, dynamic situation[…], which can be characterized by an overload of incomplete and sometimes conflicting information" (Sadiq, Kapucu et al. 2020: 66).

Finally, as the public was still feeling the effects of the COVID-19 pandemic, politicians' public brand image and identity traits were likely to be central in their ability to appeal to and connect with members of the public, as well as mobilize and strengthen their base of support (Ceccobelli and Gregorio 2022; Van Steenburg and Guzmán 2019). This chapter examines how O'Toole—and his team—structured his image-making and voter appeal efforts around aspects of his personal identity, character profile and experiences to distinguish himself from his opponents and spotlight his qualifications and readiness to take power and confront crisis situations.[1] It does so by taking an interest in O'Toole's self-image on the visual-central social media platform Instagram and through the review of CPC campaign documentation, including its electoral platform.

IDENTITY MARKETING AND PARTY LEADER BRAND IMAGE

While political and policy debates as well as party ideologies remain core components of election campaign discourse, recent studies have indicated they no longer represent the main persuasive elements of the electoral discourse and are less likely to drive the campaign news coverage (e.g., Mason 2018: 807; Zoizner 2021). As noted by Kreiss, Lawrence et al. (2020: 2), "the policy information that campaigns provide is secondary to how candidates and parties perform their" personal, partisan and social identities to reach out to and secure the support of the public. In other words, politicians' personal (e.g., gender, race, sexual orientation, physical appearance) and professional (e.g., education, professional accomplishments) identity attributes, character profile, as well as personal histories and experiences—or their overall political brand image—play a sizable role in shaping how they and, by extension, their political and policy messages are perceived, understood, evaluated and acted upon by voters (Bennett, Malone et al. 2019; Bittner 2018; Bramlett 2021; Vescio and Schermerhorn 2021, Lalancette and Tourigny-Koné, 2017).

Of particular interest for this book chapter are patterns of identity marketing during campaigns. Marketing principles are particularly salient

---

[1] Crisis situations can be defined as "uncertain, complex, dynamic situations, which can be characterized by an overload of incomplete and sometimes conflicting information" (Sadiq, Kapucu et al. 2020: 66).

in electoral politics as the "citizen/voter in the political marketplace can be viewed in a similar context as a consumer in the commercial marketplace" (Pich and Newman 2020; see also: Marland 2016). Identity marketing can be viewed as the process through which "identity-linking" electioneering efforts are designed and rolled out by politicians and political organizations to: (1) epitomize, promote and project desirable and relatable identity traits; (2) invoke and reinforce oftentimes lifestyle-based identity preferences, standards and self-motives offering meaning, "symbolic value" and a sense of belonging among voters (Newman 2020: (3). In many ways, members of the public are more likely to be receptive and amenable to political identity marketing appeals aligned or, to a lesser degree, not in conflict with personal or professional identity markers that they value, desire, or possess. Identity cues infused into an image and message-based political outreach can serve as catalysts to forge and deepen bonds with members of the electorate, build confidence and shape attitudes and behaviors strategically (Bhattacharjee, Berger et al. 2014; Stokburger-Sauer, Ratneshwar et al. 2012; Newman 2020; McGowan, Hassan et al. 2022). This dimension of political marketing is likely to gain traction over the next decades. The progressive evolution of voters' socio-political profile coupled with transformations in the off and on—online political mediascape are indeed nudging political campaigns ever more towards a "self-actualizing" and candidate-centered campaign model (Ohme 2019; Pedersen and Rahat 2021; Raynauld and Lalancette forthcoming).

This book chapter zeroes in on how national political party leaders leverage aspects of their personal and professional identity, character traits and histories to develop and broadcast a personal brand image likely to arouse and capture the interest of and resonate with the public. As they embody their party as well as its political and policy positions nationally, their political brand image is consequential as it can have trickle-down effects on regional and local races, namely on how candidates in these political settings portray themselves, structure and articulate their messaging activities, as well as are perceived by the public (Lalancette and Raynauld with Orzai 2022). The party leader brand image—which is part of the "political brand trinity" alongside the party brand and policy brand—is of particular importance (Pich and Newman; 2020; see also: Armannsdottir, Carnell et al. 2019). It can be defined as an approach to political image-making and impression management enabling party leaders to establish and strengthen a public image "structured around *tangible* dimensions such as physical appearance, style, online and offline communication tools and actions, and also *intangible* dimensions such as lived experiences, skills, values and personality characteristics" (Pich and Newman 2020; see also: Raynauld and Lalancette 2021). Bramlett (2021) echoes that point. He notes that politicians' "personalities and life stories" help highlight their attributes and, more importantly, establish clear contrasts with their competition (Bramlett 2021: 282).

Building on work by Ceccobelli and Gregorio (2022), it can be argued the party leader's brand image rests on three complementary elements—known as the "triangle of leadership"—that have cross-cutting appeal despite the growing diversification, fragmentation, and horizontalization of political audiences: (1) "competence"; (2) "authenticity" and (3) "ordinariness". First, party leaders reinforce their competence by portraying themselves as "expert[s], experienced, knowledgeable, qualified, skilled, intelligent, hardworking, with a sense of purpose, committed and with specific abilities on something" (Ceccobelli and Gregorio 2022: 114). They can turn to different tactics to demonstrate their competence. For example, their messaging can focus on their handling or mastery of specific political issues—known as "competence ownership" (Lachat 2014: 728)—or by emphasizing some of their personality traits associated with competence, including "the characteristics 'a genuine intellectual', 'an intellectual leader', 'knowledgeable', and 'well-informed'" (Aichholzer and Willmann 2020: 3). Ceccobelli and Gregorio (2022: 115) point out that party leaders can perform their competence in many ways, including spotlighting "extraordinary qualities" making them better than other politicians and "the electoral base".

Second, as politicking is becoming increasingly personalized, party leaders emphasize their authenticity to their supporters and the public at large (Luebke and Engelmann 2022; Rahat 2022). The demonstration of authenticity—which is highly performative in nature (Luebke 2021)—is twofold. On the one hand, party leaders need to show coherence and stability in their message and their actions or, in other words, stay "true to themselves […] across time and situations" (Luebke and Engelmann 2022: 4). On the other hand, they need to inject intimacy in their self-presentation and their interactions with the public. They can do so by sharing insights into elements of their personal lives or their campaign (Ceccobelli and Gregorio 2022; Lubcke 2021; Luebke and Engelmann 2022). Lastly, party leaders are expected to display some levels of ordinariness to connect with the public's day-to-day life and counterbalance their demonstration of competence. In this sense, ordinariness is viewed as politicians' ability to de-emphasize their elite background and present a more "down-to-earth" and imperfect or less polished version of themselves (Ceccobelli and Gregorio 2022; Luebke 2021).

The Appeal of Hyper–Masculinity in Politics

The interplay of image management, identity marketing and political branding represents an important component of candidates' strategy when developing and rolling out their public political brand image, which has become a central component of voter appeal (Marland 2016; Lalancette 2018). As politicians can leverage strategically facets of their personal and professional identity, character traits and histories when campaigning, this book chapter examines the role of gender identity in party leader brand image-making and impression management. In this context, gender is defined as "a multidimensional construct that refers to different roles, responsibilities, limitations, and experiences of individuals based on their presenting sex and/or gender" (Eklund, Barry et al. 2017).

While women have been increasingly influential in local, provincial and national politics in Canada, white men are still playing an outsized role[2] (e.g., Raman-Wilms 2021; Sullivan 2021). According to the Inter-Parliamentary Union (2019), 26.9% of House of Commons of Canada members and 46.7% of Senate members were women in February 2019. More recently, roughly 30% of members of the House of Commons were women in the 44th Canadian Parliament that was elected on September 20, 2021 (Raman-Wilms 2021). As of 2022, only one woman has risen to the top of the Canadian governmental hierarchy: the Progressive Conservative Party's Kim Campbell was appointed prime minister in June 1993 after winning a leadership race against former Prime Minister Brian Mulroney. In November 1993, she ran unsuccessfully to become prime minister of Canada (see: Mendelsohn and Nadeau 1999).

---

[2] It should be noted that non-normative politicians—such as members of the 2SLGBTQI + community and others with an intersectional identity profile—are far less present and visible in the political landscape (see: Tremblay 2019; Maiolino 2018).

Many studies have shown that socio-demographic and cultural elements associated with the masculine dominance paradigm—or hyper-masculinity—are influential in shaping how the public perceives and makes sense of political leaders' capacities and performance (e.g., Bashevkin 2009; Wagner, Trimble et al. 2019). Candidates during elections are expected to show more masculine traits by being "tough, combative and competitive" and possess "agentic characteristics", making female politicians face a "double bind" when posing as too assertive or too accommodating (Gidengil, Dumitrescu and Stolle 2019: 207). Lemarier-Saulnier and Giasson (2019) note that masculine characteristics can also shape how political actors are framed and evaluated by journalistic organizations.

Many scholars have drilled down on the effects of gender-infused political norms on women candidates' image-making, brand-building and voter outreach during elections (e.g.: Carpinella and Bauer 2021; Sanghvi 2019; Winfrey and Schnoebelen 2019), especially on social media (e.g., Cardo 2021; Hrbková and Macková 2021). The work of others has focused on gender's impact on public political opinion and expectations (Branton, English et al. 2018; Cassidy and Liebenow 2021). In line with these studies, Gidengil (2019: 248) argues that "even men who conform to the white, heteronormative male norm risk ridicule if they fail to exemplify hegemonic masculinity". Of particular interest is former PLC leader Micheal Ignatieff who was branded as an "American outsider" and as an academic and intellectual with a penchant for compromise and with no strength in CPC political ads during the 2006 Canadian federal elections (Marland 2015: 22; see also: Lalancette and Cormack 2020; Rose 2012). More recently, Justin Trudeau has been feminized through references to his youth and some of his physical traits (e.g. long hair) in an attempt to weaken him politically and portray him as not having the leadership skills to be prime minister (Sabin and Kirkup, 2019; Lalancette and Cormack, 2018). These critics can be situated within the hegemonic masculinity framework where "men play a role in a larger project ritualizing, naturalizing, and reproducing dominant forms of masculinity, in the process of subordinating women and feminized men" (Sabin and Kirkup 2019: 47). Few studies have examined the ways in which male politicians leverage heteronormative identity cues, character traits and experiences to promote their political brand image and leadership capacities. Specifically, while some investigations provide valuable observations, few offer a more systematic assessment of how masculinity is leveraged for political marketing (see: Wagner and Everitt 2019).

This paper focuses on how CPC's Erin O'Toole exploited his masculinity features to his advantage when defining his leadership. The academic literature on leadership gives great importance to gender stereotypes, "whether in discussions about charismatic leadership, leadership trait theory, or more contextual/situational approaches" (Waylen 2021: 1157–1158; see also: Johnson and Lacerenza 2018). On the one hand, toughness, aggressiveness, coerciveness, self-confidence and assertiveness—which can be infused in politicians' visual image-making and campaign messaging—are traits often associated with more masculine leaders. On the other hand, compassion, kindness and sensitivity tend to be linked to femininity (Gidengil, Everitt and Banducci, 2009; Jungblut and Jaim 2021). As noted by Waylen (2021: 1159), "hyper-masculine leadership is not monolithic, but contextually specific". Of particular importance is how hypermasculine features can help politicians demonstrate their readiness to hold elected office in moments of crisis and uncertainty, including economic downturns, environmental disasters, public health emergencies or national security threats. Indeed, some segments of the political market can be swayed by politicians exhibiting masculine traits as they can be perceived as better equipped for taking on these types of situations than leaders with more feminine leadership traits (Waylen 2021; 1663; Wu, Shao et al. 2021). Many studies have shown that rigidity and assertiveness—characteristics associated to the heteronormative framework—are desirable traits in crisis situations (Bundy, Pfarrer et al. 2017: 1663; see also Wu, Shao et al. 2021).

If women in politics face stereotypical assessment and are evaluated through a masculine norm, what about male politicians emphasizing masculinity in their brand image during campaigns? Raphael (2019: 127) observes that "[s]ucessfully performing hegemonic masculinity can bolster a politician's image, while failing to perform it convincingly can prove detrimental". Using O'Toole's approach to political image-making and impression management during the 2021 Canadian federal elections as a case study, this chapter spotlights how he played up the hyper-masculine facets of his public brand image to create a political ethos out-masculinizing and, by extension, standing out from the two other major-party leaders, Justin Trudeau and Jagmeet Singh. This chapter focuses on visual framing, which is central to political campaigns and often used to promote the leadership qualities and potential policy positions

(Grabe and Bucy 2009). In order to do so, this book chapter considered the CPC's magazine-style electoral document laying out all campaign promises and priorities as well as posts shared on O'Toole's personal Instagram feed throughout the electoral contest.

"The Man with a Plan"

Masculinity and masculinization strategies were front and center in the CPC's O'Toole's image-making and impression management strategies throughout 2021. It was especially the case in the CPC's magazine-style electoral platform document released publicly on August 16, 2021, in the early days of the campaign. The document—which essentially rolled out O'Toole's political leader brand image—visually highlighted his health, strength and power. It comprised catchy titles summing up the CPC's campaign priorities, including "Recover 1,000,000 JOBS" to "Canada's mental health plan action" and "New Anti-Corruption Laws".

As shown in Fig. 4.2, this document helped O'Toole introduce himself as "the man with the plan" at the outset of the campaign. His gender identity was emphasized in all dimensions of the cover page of the campaign document, from the textual content to his visual self-presentation, including his posture, the positioning of his arms and his focus on the camera. His masculinity is spotlighted through his muscular arms and pectoral muscles that are emphasized by the fitted t-shirt. The plan describes how O'Toole and the CPC can help Canadians rebound from the pandemic-induced crisis. The cover page highlights issues relating to economic priorities, including creating jobs and balancing the budget, which were at the top of Canadians' concerns at the dropping of the writ on August 14, 2021 (CTV News/Nanos 2021; Kishchuk 2021).

O'Toole's leadership is reinforced through references to aspects of his gender identity in the 87-page document. For example, 11th of the 49 pictures used to illustrate wide-ranging political and policy issues and promises (e.g., agriculture, employment) feature the CPC political leader. For the most part, he appears alone or with members of his family, which is in line with heteronormative principles. For example, he is shown with his wife, two children and a dog in outdoor settings, running with a CPC baseball cap, posing for the camera, or working and taking notes. In many respects, his gender identity and political identity are fused throughout the document which promotes the priorities and the promises of the CPC and links them to heteronormative principles.

4 THE HYPER-MASCULINE CAMPAIGN: PARTY LEADER ...   53

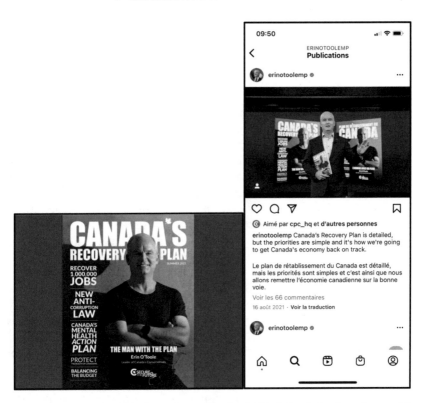

Fig. 4.2 CPC Party Platform Cover for the 2021 federal elections featured in an Instagram post by O'Toole on August 16, 2021

Emphasizing Masculinity Attributes: Tough and Ready to Fight

O'Toole and his team also showed how masculinity was an integral part of his pre-political life to reinforce his leadership brand centered around strength, resilience and toughness. O'Toole became a member of the Canadian Forces in 1991 and was named Royal Canadian Air Force officer after graduating from the Royal Military College of Canada in 1995. He left the military in 2000 and became a lawyer after completing his studies at Dalhousie University in Halifax.[3] Despite serving in the Canadian military for a relatively short period of time, it constituted a core element of his visual appeal on social media—especially on Instagram—during the 2021 campaign. As shown in Fig. 4.3, his service was used to establish a clear contrast with Trudeau's younger life. In many ways, this helped to contrast O'Toole's more masculine, experienced and strong leadership with Trudeau who has been portrayed as a more youthful, feminine political leader lacking credibility and toughness (Sabin and Kirkup 2019; Lalancette and Cormack 2018; see also: Musial and Mintz 2021). The visuals of the post are of particular interest. They show O'Toole wearing a Canadian army uniform in front of a search and rescue helicopter. While it emphasizes the seriousness and importance of his past military work, it spotlights specific facets of O'Toole's hypermasculinity that can be associated with his political leadership, including his stamina, confidence, strength, composure and rigorousness (Fig. 4.3).

In other Instagram posts (see Figs. 4.4 and 4.5), his military service is also leveraged to highlight his commitment to Canadians and his history of giving back to Canadian society. In this context, O'Toole's military service showcases his strong persona and distinguishes him from his rivals who did not serve in the military. These appeals are designed to place him in a political category—which has a strong gender connotation—of his own.

The theme of O'Toole being a strong leader is reinforced in many other Instagram posts. As demonstrated in Fig. 4.6, the visuals give the impression that O'Toole is walking towards the camera as if he just stepped out of the search and rescue helicopter following a mission. Three highly gendered words are used in the image's caption: "Tough, Tested, Ready". In many ways, O'Toole is fusing toughness, military service and political leadership. He is giving off the impression of a competent politician who has been tested under pressure and is ready to fight for Canadians, especially in a context of crisis. In sum, the military imagery is mobilized to brand the CPC leader as the quintessential masculine leader. Interestingly, O'Toole is shown with sneakers and his hands in his pants' pockets, which points to a certain level of casualness, reinforces his ordinariness and increasing his capacity to relate with members of the public (see: Ceccobelli and Gregorio 2022).

---

[3] https://lop.parl.ca/sites/ParlInfo/default/fr_CA/Personnes/Profil?personId=18117.

Fig. 4.3 Instagram Post showing O'Toole in action when he was an army pilot published during the campaign

Also of interest are the captions of the pictures included in the Instagram posts featured in Fig. 4.7 and Fig. 4.8. In both cases, they comprise war-related terminology reinforcing a very masculine vision of political leadership. They frame him as ready to "fight tirelessly for mental health, for better services, for lower prices, for more jobs". Figure 4.8 features an Instagram post with a picture showing O'Toole in a suit and tie looking at the camera, with the sentence "I will fight for you" superimposed in capital letters with Erin O'Toole signature at the bottom. The signature evokes a contract between the leader and the citizens. The commitment to fighting can be viewed as reinforcing the masculine and war registry and imaginary.

Another Instagram post (Fig. 4.9) portrays O'Toole in a jacket and waving at members of the public during a campaign event. The slogan "Secure the Future" is superimposed on the picture. In times of economic and public health uncertainty, references to securing the

Fig. 4.4 Caption of an Instagram Post showing O'Toole in action when he was an army pilot published during the campaign

future are designed to comfort voters. Again, gender is a central component of O'Toole's approach to public political leader image branding and messaging.

Strength and masculinity are showcased in Fig. 4.10 where O'Toole is shown jogging outdoors. He is wearing shorts and a t-shirt emphasizing his muscles. His running shirt and cap are red, a colour linked to the Canadian flag and the CPC's visual brand. As Grabe and Bucy argue (2009), sports are often used by politicians to promote their ordinariness and relatability as well as to create and strengthen their bonds with citizens/electors. The images of O'Toole jogging with others shared on his Instagram feed throughout the 2021 campaign are part of a marketing effort to define him as the masculine candidate in a context where the COVID-19 pandemic impacted negatively the Canadian health system and the economy. In similar ways, he was pictured wearing a cowboy hat (Fig. 4.11), which epitomizes the quintessential masculine figure (Trujillo 1911). Finally, his masculinity was anchored in normality and

Fig. 4.5 Instagram Post showing O'Toole in action when he was an army pilot shared during the campaign

heteronormativity as he was presented as a traditional family man in Instagram posts whether on the campaign trail or in more private moments (see Fig. 4.12 as an example). This places him in the triangle of leadership as the authentic and ordinary political leader (Ceccobelli and Di Gregorio, 2022). Having a more traditional family (2 parents, 2 kids and a dog), which is considered by social standards, can be seen as showing his authenticity.

58 M. LALANCETTE AND V. RAYNAULD

Fig. 4.6 Instagram post showing O'Toole in front of a Canada search and rescue helicopter shared during the campaign

Fig. 4.7 Instagram post showing O'Toole's campaign promises shared during the campaign

Fig. 4.8 Instagram post showing O'Toole promises posted during the campaign

4 THE HYPER-MASCULINE CAMPAIGN: PARTY LEADER … 61

Fig. 4.9 Caption of O'Toole Instagram account with the slogan secure the future posted during the campaign

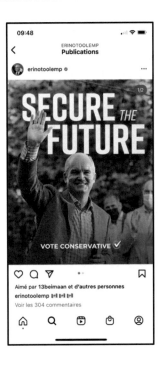

Fig. 4.10 Instagram post picturing O'Toole jogging shared on during the campaign

4 THE HYPER-MASCULINE CAMPAIGN: PARTY LEADER ... 63

Fig. 4.11 Instagram post picturing O'Toole with a cowboy hat

Fig. 4.12 Instagram post picturing O'Toole with his family advocating for the welfare of animals

Conclusion

This chapter unpacks ways in which O'Toole—and his team—developed a brand-making and voter appeal effort mobilizing aspects of his gender identity traits, character profile and experiences to distinguish himself from his opponents and spotlight his qualifications and readiness to take power. The analysis of the textual and visual materials considered in his study—including his magazine-style campaign platform as well as his Instagram-based updates—revealed that hypermasculinity-related visual and textual cues were leveraged to market the CPC leader and his party in specific and strategic ways, especially in a context of health and economic crisis in Canada.

In all aspects of the campaign marketing appeals considered for this study, O'Toole and his team used his gender identity through references to his military career and other accomplishments to foster an impression of strength, stamina, power, and ability to fight among the public. All appeals emphasized the fact that O'Toole could be seen as a trusted leader ready to hold the elected office that was more likely to address the issues plaguing the country than his opponents. Interestingly, O'Toole's campaign message blended aspects of gender, political leadership and policy promises to connect with the Canadian audience as well as distinguish himself from other political appeals. Masculinity was the identity trait that was promoted during the campaign (Newman 2020). Following Ceccobelli and DiGregorio's work on leadership (2022), by leveraging identity and his career in the military, O'Toole placed himself in the triangle of leadership exceptionality status, while also creating an authentic and ordinary self when presenting his personal life with his quintessential heteronormative family of four, plus a dog.

This political leadership image brand positioning differentiated him from all other leaders and helped him put forth an appeal that was adapted to the context of the pandemic crisis in Canada. Despite O'Toole's approach, O'Toole's campaign was not successful as the CPC came in second position. The CPC secured 118 seats in the House of Commons (34.9% of all seats). While his political appeal likely helped him secure the support of some segments of the public, it was not enough to secure enough votes to beat Trudeau's LPC. Does this election outcome mean that identity marketing based on gender is not a viable electioneering strategy? More research is needed to unpack this question further. Building on existing political marketing and communication literature, there is no doubt that gender is an integral element of campaign political marketing communication, especially in a context where identity is playing an increasingly impotent role in politics (Busby 2014; Sanghvi 2019). Future work will be consecrated to these issues following the work of these authors and also the other academics that we referred to in this chapter.

References

Aichholzer, J., & Willmann, J. (2020). Desired personality traits in politicians: Similar to me but more of a leader. *Journal of Research in Personality, 88*, 103990.

Aiello, R. (2022). O'Toole resigns as Conservative leader, will stay on as MP, *CTV News.* https://www.ctvnews.ca/politics/o-toole-resigns-as-conservative-leader-will-stay-on-as-mp-1.574196.

Armannsdottir, G. Carnell, S. & Pich, C. (2019). Exploring personal politic brands of Iceland's parliamentarians, *Journal of Political Marketing*, 19(1/2).

Anderson, B., & Coletto, D. (2021). As the campaign kicks off, Liberals lead by 5 over Conservatives as the NDP rises to 22%, *Abascus Data*, https://abacusdata.ca/election-2021-liberal-lead-shrinks/.

Austen, I. (2021). How Canadian leaders campaign in a pandemic. *The New York Times*. https://www.nytimes.com/2021/08/27/world/canada/canada-leaders-campaign-pandemic.html.

Bhattacharjee, A., Berger, J., & Menon, G. (2014). When identity marketing backfires: Consumer agency in identity expression. *Journal of Consumer Research*, 41(2), 294–309.

Bennett, A. M., Malone, C., Cheatham, K., & Saligram, N. (2019). The impact of perceptions of politician brand warmth and competence on voting intentions. *Journal of Product & Brand Management*, 28(2).

Bashevkin, S. (2009) *Women, power, politics: The hidden story of Canada's unfinished democracy*. Oxford: Oxford University Press.

Bittner, A. (2018). Leaders always mattered: The persistence of personality in Canadian elections. *Electoral Studies*, 54, 297–302.

Bolton, J. P. (2022). I'm in: Presidential campaign announcement speeches among well known and unknown candidates. *Atlantic Journal of Communication*, 1–13.

Bouchard, J. (2022). I think Canadians look like all sorts of people: Ethnicity, political leadership, and the case of Jagmeet Singh. *Journal of Race, Ethnicity, and Politics*, 7(2), 316–347.

Bramlett, J. C. (2021). Battles for branding: A political marketing approach to studying televised candidate debates. *Communication Quarterly*, 69(3), 280–300.

Branton, R., English, A., Pettey, S., & Barnes, T. D. (2018). The impact of gender and quality opposition on the relative assessment of candidate competency. *Electoral Studies*, 54, 35–43.

Bryden, J. (2021). All parties modifying, scrapping usual campaign tools to avoid spreading COVID-19, *CTV News*. https://www.ctvnews.ca/politics/federal-election-2021/all-parties-modifying-scrapping-usual-campaign-tools-to-avoid-spreading-covid-19-1.5547933.

Bundy, J., Pfarrer, M. D., Short, C. E., & Coombs, W. T. (2017). Crises and crisis management: Integration, interpretation, and research development. Journal of Management, 43(6), 1661–1692.

Busby, R. (2014). Mama Grizzlies: Republican female candidates and the political marketing dilemma. In Lees-Marshment, J., Conley, B., & Cosgrove, K. (Eds.). *Political marketing in the United States* (pp. 220–237). New York: Routledge.

Cassidy, B. S., & Liebenow, H. A. (2021). Feminine perceptions of Kamala Harris positively relate to evaluations of her candidacy. *Analyses of Social Issues and Public Policy*, 21(1), 29–50.

CBC News (2021). Éric Grenier's Poll Tracker. *CBC News*. https://newsinteractives.cbc.ca/elections/poll-tracker/canada/.

Cardo, V. (2021). Gender politics online? Political women and social media at election time in the United Kingdom, the United States and New Zealand. *European Journal of Communication*, 36(1), 38–52.

Canzi, E., Danioni, F.V., Parise, M., Lopez, G., Ferrari, L., Ranieri, S., Iafrate, R., Lanz, M., Regalia, C. and Rosnati, R. (2021). Perceived changes in family life during COVID-19: The role of family size. *Family Relations*, 70(5), 1303–1311.

Carpinella, C., & Bauer, N. M. (2021). A visual analysis of gender stereotypes in campaign advertising. *Politics, Groups, and Identities*, 9(2), 369–386.

Carroll, S. & Fox, R. L. (2006) *Gender and elections: Shaping the future of American Politics*. Cambridge: Cambridge University Press.

Carson, J. L., Sievert, J., & Williamson, R. D. (2020). Nationalization and the incumbency advantage. *Political Research Quarterly*, 73(1), 156–168.

Ceccobelli, D., & Di Gregorio, L. (2022). The triangle of leadership. Authenticity, competence and ordinariness in political marketing. *Journal of Political Marketing*, 21(2), 113–125.

CTV News/Nanos. (2021).The economy rates as top policy issue that will influence vote in a potential fall election. *CTV News/Nano*. https://nanos.co/wp-content/uploads/2021/07/2021-1917-CTV-June-Populated-report-POWERPLAY-with-tabs.pdf.

Crandall, E., & Roy, M. (2020). Party Fundraisers. In Marland, A. & Giasson, T. (Eds.) (2020). *Inside the campaign: Managing elections in Canada* Vancouver: UBC Press.

Da Vinha, L., & Ernst, N. (2018). The unfinished presidencies: why incumbent presidents may lose their re-election bids. *Perspectivas*, 18, 7.

Eklund, K. E., Barry, E. S., & Grunberg, N. E. (2017). Gender and leadership. In Alvinius, A. (2017) (Ed.) *Gender differences in different contexts*. London: IntechOpen.

Elections Canada (2021). Campaign guidance for canvassing during COVID-19. Elections Canada. https://www.elections.ca/content.aspx?section=pol&document=index&dir=can/pand&lang=e.

Faulkner, G., Rhodes, R. E., Vanderloo, L. M., Chulak-Bozer, T., O'Reilly, N., Ferguson, L., & Spence, J. C. (2020). Physical activity as a coping strategy for mental health due to the COVID-19 virus: A potential disconnect among Canadian adults? *Frontiers in Communication*, 5, 571833.

Fuller, S., & Qian, Y. (2021). Covid-19 and the gender gap in employment among parents of young children in Canada. *Gender & Society*, 35(2), 206–217.

Gidengil, E., Everitt, J., & Banducci, S. (2009). Do voters stereotype female party leaders? Evidence from Canada and New Zealand. In *Opening doors wider, women's political engagement in Canada*, Vancouver : UBC-Press, pp. 167–193.

Gidengil, E., Dumitrescu, D., Stolle, D. (2019). Gender and candidate communication. Is there a "double bind?" in *Gendered mediation. Identity and images in Canadian Politics* edited by Angelia Wagner and Joanna Everitt, Vancouver: UBC Press, pp. 207–226.

Gidengil, E. (2019). The complexity of gendered identities in Canadian politics. In *Gendered Mediation. Identity and images in Canadian Politics* edited by Angelia Wagner and Joanna Everitt, Vancouver: UBC Press, pp. 247–264.

Grabe M. E., & Bucy E. P. (2009). *Image bite politics: News and the visual framing of elections*. Oxford: Oxford University Press.

Hrbková, L., & Macková, A. (2021). Campaign like a girl? Gender and communication on social networking sites in the Czech Parliamentary election. *Information, Communication & Society*, 24(11), 1622–1639

Inter-Parliamentary Union (2019). Women in national parliaments. *Inter-Parliamentary Union*. http://archive.ipu.org/wmn-e/classif.htm.

Johnson, S. K., & Lacerenza, C. N. (2018). Leadership is male-centric: Gender issues in the study of leadership. In Rioggio, R. E. (Ed.) (2018) *What's wrong with leadership?* New York: Routledge.

Jungblut, M., & Haim, M. (2021). Visual gender stereotyping in campaign communication: evidence on female and male candidate imagery in 28 countries. *Communication Research*. https://doi.org/00936502211023333.

Kishchuk, O. (2021). Election Bulletin: Top issues for men vs. women in this election. *Abacus Data*. https://abacusdata.ca/election-gender-equality/.

Kreiss, D., Lawrence, R. G., & McGregor, S. C. (2020). Political identity ownership: Symbolic contests to represent members of the public. *Social Media + Society*, 6(2). https://doi.org/2056305120926495.

Lachat, R. (2014). Issue ownership and the vote: The effects of associative and competence ownership on issue voting. *Swiss Political Science Review*, 20(4), 727–740.

Lalancette, M., & Raynauld, V. (2020). Politicking and Visual Framing on Instagram: A Look at the Portrayal of the Leadership of Canada's Justin Trudeau. *Études canadiennes/Canadian Studies. Revue interdisciplinaire des études canadiennes en France*, (89), 257–290.

Lalancette, M. & Tourigny-Koné, S. (2017). 24 Seven Videostyle: Blurring the Lines and Building Strong Leadership. Dans A. Marland, T. Giasson &

A. Esselment (dir.) Permanent Campaigning in Canada (pp. 259–277). Vancouver: UBC Press.

Lalancette, M. (2018). Les web-mises en scène des candidats aux élections québécoises de 2012: entre discrétion et confession. *Politique et société, 37*(2): 47–81.

Lawson, T., L. Nathans et al. (2022). COVID-19: Recovery and re-opening tracker. McCarthy Tetrault. https://www.mccarthy.ca/en/insights/articles/covid-19-recovery-and-re-opening-tracker.

Leger. (2021a). Leger North American Tracker: August 2, 2021a. Leger. https://2g2ckk18vixp3neolz4b6605-wpengine.netdna-ssl.com/wp-content/uploads/2021/08/Legers-North-American-Tracker-August-2nd-2021_v2.pdf.

Leger. (2021b). Leger North American Tracker: August 16, 2021b. Leger. https://2g2ckk18vixp3neolz4b6605-wpengine.netdna-ssl.com/wp-content/uploads/2021/08/Legers-North-American-Tracker-August-16th-2021.pdf.

Lemarier-Saulnier, C. & Giasson, T. (2019) She's too tough and he's too soft. Measuring how gender news frames affect voter's evaluation of party leaders, In *Gendered mediation. Identity and images in Canadian Politics* edited by Angelia Wagner and Joanna Everitt, Vancouver: UBC Press, pp. 185–206.

Lemieux, T., Milligan, K., Schirle, T., & Skuterud, M. (2020). Initial impacts of the COVID-19 pandemic on the Canadian labour market. *Canadian Public Policy, 46*(S1), S55–S65.

Lalancette, M., & Cormack, P. (2020). Justin Trudeau and the play of celebrity in the 2015 Canadian federal election campaign. *Celebrity Studies, 11*(2), 157–170.

Luebke, S. M. (2021). Political authenticity: Conceptualization of a popular term. *The International Journal of Press/Politics, 26*(3), 635–653.

Luebke, S. M., & Engelmann, I. (2022). Do we know politicians' true selves from the media? Exploring the relationship between political media exposure and perceived political authenticity. *Social Media + Society, 8*(1). https://doi.org/20563051221077030.

Mainstreet Research. (2021). "Mainstreet/Toronto Star - LPC: 35% - CPC: 29% - NDP: 18% - BQ: 6% - GPC: 5%." *Mainstreet Research.* https://www.mainstreetresearch.ca/poll/mainstreet-toronto-star-lpc-35-cpc-29-ndp-18-bq-6-gpc-5/.

Maiolino, E. (2018). I'm not male, not white, want to start there?: Olivia Chow and identity work in Toronto's 2014 Mayoral Election. *Journal of Women, Politics & Policy, 39*(2), 220–245.

Marland, A. (2015). Going negative: Campaigning in Canadian provinces. *Canadian Political Science Review, 9*(1), 14–27.

Marland, A. (2016). *Brand command: Canadian politics and democracy in the age of message control.* UBC Press.

Marland, A. (2018). The brand image of Canadian Prime Minister Justin Trudeau in international context. *Canadian Foreign Policy, 29*(2), 139–144.

Marshall, J., Roache, D., & Moody-Marshall, R. (2020). Crisis leadership: A critical examination of educational leadership in higher education in the midst of the COVID-19 pandemic. *International Studies in Educational Administration (Commonwealth Council for Educational Administration & Management), 48*(3), 30–37.

Mason, L. (2018). Ideologues without issues: The polarizing consequences of ideological identities. *Public Opinion Quarterly, 82*(S1), 866–887.

McGowan, M., Hassan, L. M., & Shiu, E. (2022). Examining the effect of group prototypes and divergent strength of identification on the effectiveness of identity appeals. *European Journal of Marketing*.

McLean, J. (2021). Gliding in on a wing and a prayer: Jagmeet Singh and the NDP. In Gillies, J. Raynauld, V. & Turcotte, A. (2021) *Political marketing in the 2019 Canadian federal election* (pp. 41–55). Palgrave Pivot, Cham.

Metcalfe, A. S. (2021). Visualizing the COVID-19 pandemic response in Canadian higher education: An extended photo essay. *Studies in Higher Education, 46*(1), 5–18.

Mendelsohn, M., & Nadeau, R. (1999). The rise and fall of candidates in Canadian election campaigns. *Harvard International Journal of Press/Politics, 4*(2), 63–76.

Musial, J., & Mintz, J. (2021). Because It's 2015!: Justin Trudeau's yoga body, masculinity, and Canadian nation-building. *Journal of Feminist Scholarship, 18*(18), 24–42

Newman, T. P. (2020). The emergence of science as a political brand. *Journal of Political Marketing, 19*(1-2), 137–152.

Ohme, J. (2019). Updating citizenship? The effects of digital media use on citizenship understanding and political participation. *Information, Communication & Society, 22*(13), 1903–1928.

Pedersen, H. H., & Rahat, G. (2021). Political personalization and personalized politics within and beyond the behavioural arena. *Party Politics, 27*(2), 211–219.

Pich, C., & Newman, B. I. (2020). Evolution of political branding: Typologies, diverse settings and future research. *Journal of Political Marketing, 19*(1-2), 3–14.

Rahat, G. (2022). Party types in the age of personalized politics. *Perspectives on Politics*, 1–16.

Raman-Wilms, M. (2021). Trudeau promises another gender balanced cabinet, but parity in the House is still far off, *The globe and Mail*. https://www.theglobeandmail.com/politics/article-trudeau-promises-another-gender-balanced-cabinet-but-parity-in-the/.

Raphael, D. (2019). May the best man win. Masculinity in Canadian political humour. In *Gendered mediation. Identity and images in Canadian Politics* edited by Angelia Wagner and Joanna Everitt, Vancouver: UBC Press, pp. 127–144.

Raynauld, V., & Lalancette, M. (2021). Pictures, filters, and politics: Instagram's role in political image making and storytelling in Canada. *Visual Communication Quarterly, 28*(4), 212–226.

Raynauld, V. & Lalancette, M. (forthcoming). Social media, visuals, and politics: A look at the digital visual habitus on Instagram. In Veneti, A. and D. Lilleker (Ed.) (forthcoming). *Research handbook on visual politics.* Edward Elgar.

Rose, J. (2012). Are negative ads positive? Political advertising and the permanent campaign. In Taras, D. and Waddell, C. (Eds.), *How Canadians communicate IV: Media and politics.* Athabasca University Press, Athabasca, AB.

Sabin, J., & Kirkup, K. (2019). Competing masculinities and political campaigns. In *Gendered Mediation. Identity and images in Canadian Politics* edited by Angelia Wagner and Joanna Everitt, Vancouver: UBC Press, pp. 45–64.

Sadiq, A. A., Kapucu, N., & Hu, Q. (2020). Crisis leadership during COVID-19: The role of governors in the United States. *International Journal of Public Leadership. 17*(1), 65–80.

Sanghvi, M. (2019). Gender and intersectionality in political marketing. In Sanghvi, M. (2019) *Gender and political marketing in the United States and the 2016 presidential election.* Cham: Palgrave Macmillan.

Sanghvi, M. (Ed.) (2019). *Gender and political marketing in the United States and the 2016 presidential election. Gender and politics: An analysis of why she lost.* Palgrave Macmillan, Cham. https://doi.org/10.1007/978-1-137-60171-1_1

Stokburger-Sauer, N., Ratneshwar, S., & Sen, S. (2012). Drivers of consumer–brand identification. *International Journal of Research in Marketing, 29*(4), 406–418.

Statistics Canada. (2021). COVID-19 in Canada: A one-year update on social and economic impacts, *Statistics Canada.* https://www150.statcan.gc.ca/n1/pub/11-631-x/11-631-x2021001-eng.htm#a4.

Sullivan, K. V. (2021). The gendered digital turn: Canadian mayors on social media. *Information Polity, 26*(2), 157-171.

Theviot, A. (2016). «Rôle» politique et modelage des identités de genre. du candidat au président: mise en scène virtuelle des masculinités de François Hollande. *Genre en séries. Cinéma, télévision, médias,* (3), 45–74.

Tremblay, M. (2019) *Queering representation. LGBTQ people and electoral politics in Canada.* Vancouver: UBC Press.

Trujillo, N. (1991). Hegemonic masculinity on the mound: Media representations of Nolan Ryan and American sports culture. *Critical Studies in Media Communication, 8*(3), 290308.

Van Steenburg, E., & Guzmán, F. (2019). The influence of political candidate brands during the 2012 and 2016 U.S. presidential elections. *European Journal of Marketing*.

Vescio, T. K., & Schermerhorn, N. E. (2021). Hegemonic masculinity predicts 2016 and 2020 voting and candidate evaluations. *Proceedings of the National Academy of Sciences, 118*(2), e2020589118.

Wagner, A., Trimble, L., & Sampert, S. (2019). One smart politician: gendered media discourses of political leadership in Canada. *Canadian Journal of Political Science/Revue canadienne de science politique, 52*(1), 141–162.

Wagner, A., & Everitt, J. (Eds.) (2019). *Gendered mediation. Identity and images in Canadian Politics* edited by Angelia Wagner and Joanna Everitt, Vancouver: UBC Press.

Waylen, G. (2021). Gendering political leadership: Hypermasculine leadership and Covid-19. *Journal of European Public Policy, 28*(8), 1153–1173.

Winfrey, K. L., & Schnoebelen, J. M. (2019). Running as a woman (or man): A review of research on political communicators and gender stereotypes. *Review of Communication Research, 7*, 109–138.

Wu, Y. L., Shao, B., Newman, A., & Schwarz, G. (2021). Crisis leadership: A review and future research agenda. *The Leadership Quarterly, 32*(6), 101518.

Zoizner, A. (2021). The consequences of strategic news coverage for democracy: A meta-analysis. *Communication Research, 48*(1), 3–25.

CHAPTER 5

Le Bloc Québécois: A Niche Party

Guy Lachapelle

Abstract On August 15, 2021, the Prime Minister of Canada, Justin Trudeau, launched his troops on the election campaign. The Prime Minister of Canada made no secret of his ambition to seek a majority. Governing with the opposition parties and forming coalitions on several issues was not an optimal option for the Liberal Party. The goal of the Bloc Québécois (BQ), a sovereigntist party representing Quebec's interests in Ottawa, was to stop the ambition of the Prime Minister and get a majority of the votes from Québec voters. The Premier of Québec, François Legault, made it clear that he was supportive of the Conservative Party simply because his analysis was that the CPC had a platform closer to the Québec demands. Therefore, the Bloc had to face a wind coming from Ottawa and one coming from Québec City. To the surprise of everyone, the English debate sparked the attention of Québec voters because of the opening comments made by the moderator that Québec laws are discriminatory—especially concerning the secularism of the state.

G. Lachapelle (✉)
Department of Political Science, Concordia University, Montreal, QC, Canada
e-mail: guy.lachapelle@concordia.ca

© The Author(s), under exclusive license to Springer Nature Switzerland AG 2023
J. Gillies et al. (eds.), *Political Marketing in the 2021 Canadian Federal Election*, Palgrave Studies in Political Marketing and Management, https://doi.org/10.1007/978-3-031-34404-6_5

These remarks sparked debates over the values of Quebecers and the francophobia in the rest of Canada. This unexpected event helped the BQ to regain momentum at the end of the campaign and motivated voters to support BQ candidates. This chapter considers the BQ campaign and how its leader, Yves-François Blanchet, targeted Québec voters, especially after the English language debate. It considers the political marketing and branding strategies the BQ successfully deployed to differentiate itself from both the Liberals and Conservatives and how, once again, the BQ was able to over-perform expectations. As was the case in 2019, this was less to do with the political strategy of the BQ and more to do with a Quebec values-based marketing that emphasized linguistic and cultural brand focus to the detriment of the other campaigns.

Keywords Québec · Language · Election · Sovereignty · Bloc Québécois · Values

The analysis of the Bloc Québécois campaign in the 2021 federal election is of particular interest, especially in the wake of the 2018 Coalition avenir Québec (CAQ) government in Quebec and the election of François Legault as premier. This centre-right party, with its more autonomist vision, had succeeded in forming a majority government with 74 seats out of 125; the Quebec Liberal Party elected only 32 MPs and its support among francophone voters was significantly down. In the 2019 federal election, the Bloc Québécois with its new leader, Yves-François Blanchet, caused a surprise by electing 32 MPs and becoming a recognized party in the House of Commons. The BQ's objective in 2021 was to retain its seats from the last election and above all to dethrone the Liberal Party of Canada (LPC) in the popular vote.

For the LPC, the battle for Quebec was crucial because when Justin Trudeau launched his campaign on August 15, 2021, he made no secret of his ambition to make gains in Quebec and elsewhere in Canada to win a majority—170 out of 338—in the House of Commons. It should be noted that in the past two decades, only two of the seven elections have produced majority governments: the 2011 election won by the Conservative Stephen Harper and the 2015 election that elected the Liberal Justin Trudeau (Bélair-Cirino 2021). Since the beginning of the Canadian Confederation, five of the nine minority governments have been elected

Table 5.1 Minority Governments in Canada

1921–1925	William Lyon Mackenzie King (Parti libéral)
1925–1926	William Lyon Mackenzie King (Parti libéral)
1926	Arthur Meighen (Parti conservateur)
1957–1958	John Diefenbaker (Parti conservateur)
2004–2006	Paul Martin (Parti libéral)
2006–2008	Stephen Harper (Parti conservateur)
2008–2011	Stephen Harper (Parti conservateur)
2019–2021	Justin Trudeau (Parti libéral)
2021…	Justin Trudeau (Parti libéral)

Source Encyclopédie Canadienne

after 2004, reflecting the recent inability of federal institutions to win majority support in all provinces (see Table 5.1).

The objective of this chapter is to analyse the Bloc Québécois campaign in the particular context of an ongoing pandemic—the fourth wave of COVID-19. It is often mentioned by authors working in political communication that the link between marketing and politics is neglected or even absent from debates (Butler and Collins 1996). For these researchers, political science research tends to minimize the fact that the primary objective is to convince voters to vote for them and their party. One definition of political marketing is Clemente's: "The marketing of ideas and opinions which relate to public or political issues or to specific candidates. In general, political marketing is designed to influence people's votes in elections" (Clemente 1992). However, the techniques of persuasion used have evolved considerably over the past thirty years and many books now present the strategies used by political organizations and candidates to convince the greatest number of voters (Maarek 2011).

In the specific case of the Bloc Québécois, some consider this party to be a niche party because it presents many issues that are often absent in the discourse of other traditional political parties and the division between left and right parties (Meyer and Miller 2015). Meguid, for example, includes in his typology of niche parties that they tend to engage in debates about ethnocultural issues (Meguid 2005). Meyer and Miller's definition is to define a niche party as a "Party competing on policy areas neglected by its rivals" (2015: 267). But what is essential to understand in the case of the Bloc Québécois is that it has become over the years much more than a party promoting Quebec independence for Quebec voters. It has become an unavoidable voice for the demands of political parties in the Quebec National Assembly and deeply rooted in Quebec's political mores (Charbonneau and Lachapelle 2010).

The primary goal of the Bloc Québécois is to promote "national awareness", to be the bearer of Quebec values and to defend the interests of Quebec. Niche parties have an intrinsic value, that of wanting to go against the grain of certain preconceived ideas and myths that often inflame the ideologies of traditional parties at the pan-Canadian and federal levels. But we can also think that the Bloc Québécois is a reflection of a new culture of Quebecers towards values that are, to use Ronald Inglehart's expression, more post-materialist than materialist (Inglehart 1990). From this perspective, it is certainly possible to hypothesize that the issues debated by the BQ in its electoral platform reflect a rejection by its members of the attitude of the federal elites towards Quebec. The Bloc Québécois could thus be defined as a post-materialist centre-left party that responds to the social democratic values of Quebecers.

We will therefore try to explain how the Bloc Québécois built its communication campaign by focusing on its own issues, by aligning its discourse with the demands of the Quebec government, even though Premier François Legault gave his support to the Conservative Party, and by positioning itself as the only party in symbiosis with Quebec voters.

The Theme of the Campaign: "QUÉBÉCOIS"

At the launch of his election campaign on August 22, 2021, the leader of the Bloc Québécois, Yves-François Blanchet, emphasized that his party's objective in 2021 was to win some 40 seats and, above all, to win the ridings lost in 2019 by 1,000 votes or less. At the outset, the need for such an election was constantly questioned by the BQ leader, who believed, like many voters in Canada, that the federal parliament could function very well even with a minority government. The idea of a "hasty or unnecessary" election would haunt the entire Liberal campaign, which would have to justify the holding of this election. Clearly, the No. 1 enemy of this campaign was Justin Trudeau's Liberal Party of Canada.

The theme of the BQ campaign "Québécois" would be the leitmotif of the campaign. Beyond the public health issue that the pandemic represented, the Premier of Quebec had repeatedly indicated his dissatisfaction with the federal government's intransigence regarding health transfers and its management of immigration, particularly the entry of migrants from the United States. In addition, identity issues (language, culture, immigration) were on the legislative agenda of the Quebec government. For the Bloc, the strategy was to align itself with the CAQ's priorities while speaking to all voters in Quebec. In contrast, the Liberal Party of Canada's slogan "Let's move forward together" seemed a bit meaningless, as Justin Trudeau claimed that he called this election because he had difficulty working with the opposition parties. The priority for the BQ is Quebecers and Yves-François Blanchet added, "only Quebecers". BQ strategists also decided to hold two press briefings a day and to concentrate their efforts on ridings with Liberal members.

The BQ Election Platform and the Battle of the Suburbs

The Bloc Québécois election platform consisted of 38 proposals grouped into three themes: (1) to put an end to the pandemic ($n = 6$); (2) Quebecers, for who we are ($n = 17$); (3) Quebecers for what we want ($n = 15$). Table 5.2 presents all the themes selected. The Bloc's strategy for implementing its program was to hold press briefings twice a day, which allowed BQ leader Yves-François Blanchet to have an optimal media presence and also to react to the various events of the day. The fact that the vote for the Bloc Québécois is concentrated in Quebec obviously facilitates regional tours and allowed the leader to have a more sustained presence in several ridings and in particular in the greater Montreal area where the BQ held a large number of seats. An analysis of the travel of the leaders of the various parties during the 2019 federal campaign clearly showed that the Bloc leader held more than half of his events there, which gave him a clear advantage over his opponents (Figs. 5.1 and 5.2).

Following the very definition of a niche party, we could group the Bloc Québécois's electoral proposals into what Inglehart sees as materialist and post-materialist values. Thus all the proposals related to the pandemic and the state of the healthcare system in Quebec, including the demand for additional federal transfers for health care, could well be considered as touching on the physical and material survival or security of individuals. We should not underestimate the fact that the election campaign took place in a time frame permeated by the urgency of public decision-makers to address the COVID-19 health crisis. As for the other proposals of the BQ program, they are clearly values related to the protection of culture

Table 5.2 The 38 proposals of the Bloc Québécois

A. To put an end to the pandemic
1. Health transfer: The federal government should increase health transfers, without conditions, to cover 35% of healthcare costs. Tax credit for home care
2. Living Conditions for Seniors. Increase the monthly pension for all seniors, starting at age 65
3. International leadership on COVID-19
4. Labour shortage
5. Vaccine autonomy
6. Seasonal businesses: changes to business assistance programs

B. Quebecers, for what we are
7. French Language
8. Challenging Quebec's choices
9. Solidarity with the sick
10. Freedom of expression
11. The image of Quebec
12. Arts and culture
13. Equality of women and men
14. Combating domestic violence
15. Tax justice
16. Ethics
17. Nation to Nation Relations
18. Support for workers
19. Host Society
20. A roof for everyone
21. International relations
22. A peaceful society
23. Making our choices

C. Quebecers by what we want
24. Fighting climate change
25. Ecological transition: the GST ceases to be collected on the Hydro-Québec bills of households
26. Economic nationalism
27. Agriculture and agri-food
28. Healthy eating
29. Aerospace
30. Forestry industry
31. Clean aluminum
32. Infrastructure
33. Land development
34. Local purchasing

(continued)

Table 5.2 (continued)

35. Single Tax Report
36. Shipbuilding industry
37. St. Lawrence
38. Veterans Affairs: The Veterans Ombudsman had determined that the median processing time for Francophones was 52 weeks, compared to 19 for Anglophones

Source Bloc Québécois, *Plateforme politique—Bloc 2021*. Août 2021
https://www.blocquebecois.org/plateforme/

and the power of citizens to participate in government decisions. In the case of the BQ, as is the case with most niche parties, there is always a need to base its legitimacy on the need to have a citizen-based approach that responds to the demands of citizens, and in particular the middle class.

As of 2019, the electoral struggle was primarily in the greater Montreal area and its suburbs (Provost 2021). In order to obtain their majority of seats in Quebec, both the Bloc and the Liberals redoubled their efforts to reach out to French-speaking voters in these ridings. These include Longueuil-Saint-Hubert, Longueuil-Charles-LeMoyne, Montarville, Chateauguay-Lacolle and Shefford on the south shore of Montreal. In these ridings, many voters were critical of Justin Trudeau's decision to hold this election.

One of the characteristics of these ridings is their semi-urban character and many businesses were clearly affected by the labour shortage. For example, in the case of the riding of Joliette, on the northeast side of the greater Montreal area in the Lanaudière region, a large proportion of jobs are in the agricultural sector. According to the *Union des producteurs agricoles* (UPA), the bio-food industry generates some 22,500 jobs, of which 3,400 are directly related to agriculture (UPA 2015). It should also be noted that on its territory there is the Atikamekw of Manawan native reserve. For Bloc candidate Gabriel St-Marie, the labour shortage in the agricultural sector and the breach in supply management were issues that were at the heart of his campaign. In fact, following the renegotiations of NAFTA and the new free trade agreements with Europe and the Asia–Pacific zone, the Bloc MP had a unanimous motion adopted in the House of Commons to fully compensate producers affected by the new rules on supply management.

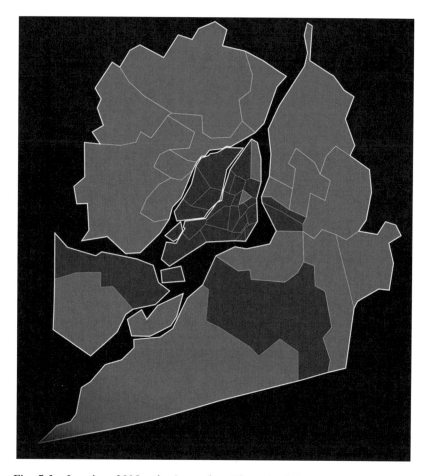

Fig. 5.1 In the 2019 election, the Bloc Québécois made significant gains in the Greater Montreal area. In 2021, the Liberals needed to take a number of seats from the BQ to form a majority government (*Source* https://ici.radio-canada.ca/info/2019/elections-federales/resultats-cartes-vainqueur-perdant-partis-circonscriptions/)

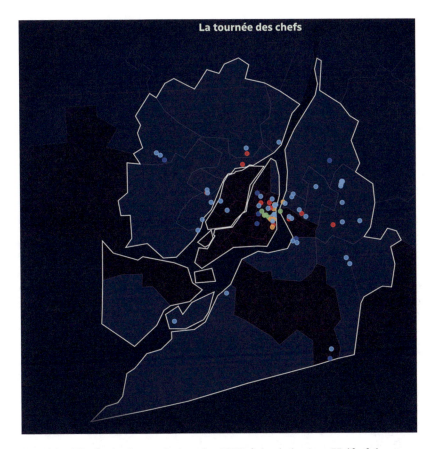

Fig. 5.2 The leaders' tour during the 2019 federal election. Half of the events held by Yves-François Blanchet, the leader of the Bloc, took place in the greater Montreal area (*Source* https://ici.radio-canada.ca/info/2019/elections-federales/resultats-cartes-vainqueur-perdant-partis-circonscriptions/)

Gabriel St-Marie's campaign focused on the Bloc's platform proposal of "suspending the Canadian Economic Recovery Benefit (CERB), encouraging the work of seniors with their invaluable expertise, allowing low-income seniors to work more without penalty and involving Aboriginal nations, as well as encouraging the settlement of newcomers and graduates in the regions" (BQ 2021: 11). The Bloc candidate insisted that the ERCP did not encourage some workers to return to the labour market and aggravated the labour shortage. He called for greater flexibility in the processing of temporary workers hired by agricultural businesses, while also calling for an improvement in the employment insurance system for seasonal workers. It is therefore not surprising that the Bloc candidate was re-elected (55% of the vote) with a majority of 12,731 votes over his closest opponent, the Liberal candidate Michel Bourgeois (22.7%).

Tie in with François Legault's Ten (10) Demands

Another central element of the campaign that somehow gave more resonance to the Bloc Québécois proposals was the letter sent at the end of August by the Premier of Quebec to the various leaders of the federal parties. François Legault asked each leader to commit to responding to the various priority demands of Quebec. For the Bloc Québécois, this intervention came at the right time, as it allowed it to increase the national fervour of voters and to bring its program into line with the demands of the leader of the Quebec government. The demands of the leader of the Coalition avenir Québec also allowed the Bloc Québécois candidates to campaign by committing to be the spokesperson for the demands of the Premier of Quebec.

The ten requests read as follows:

1. That the federal government assumes its fair share of the costs of Quebecers' health care—an increase from 22 to 35% of expenditures.
2. More power in immigration to fill labour shortages and integrate immigrants into the francophone majority.
3. Application of the Charter of the French Language to businesses under federal jurisdiction.
4. Respect for the autonomy of the Quebec people and their democratic choices in matters of secularism.
5. Modification of the structure of federal payments so that they have transferred en bloc and that they are complementary to the investments provided for in the Quebec Infrastructure Plan.
6. Respect for Quebec's jurisdiction over housing.
7. Changes to the legislative framework for environmental assessments—a single procedure for projects under Quebec's jurisdiction.

8. Block funding and transfer for Quebec climate change initiatives to support the 2030 Green Economy Plan.
9. An agreement recognizing Quebec's unconditional right to opt-out, with full financial compensation, of any federal spending in its areas of jurisdiction.
10. Implementation of a single income tax return administered by the Quebec government.

However, the leader of the Bloc Québécois, Yves-François Blanchet, was caught up in the campaign on the issue of the third road link between Quebec City and Lévis. By stating that he was in favour of this project, adding that it could even be "ecological", he drew the ire of many environmentalists and went against his proposals for greener policies (Plante 2021). The strategic mistake was to alienate a significant segment of the electorate that was willing to support him to demonstrate to Ottawa the inconsistencies in the environmental policies of Justin Trudeau's federal government, from the Alberta tar sands to the management of the climate crisis, and the Conservative Party's privileged ties to the Alberta oil industry. By intervening on a "regional" issue, the Bloc was undoubtedly hoping to get a few Conservative votes in the Quebec City area. But the calculation was disastrous and may have cost Yves-François Blanchet's party the majority of Quebec's seats it was looking for. For a party that wanted to be at the forefront of the major social debates of the day, the BQ gave the image of an electoralist and opportunist party, but above all, it went against the concerns of its electoral clientele.

François Legault's Support for the Conservative Party

At a press conference held on September 9, François Legault offered his support to the Conservatives, considering in particular that Erin O'Toole's party would not interfere in Quebec's areas of jurisdiction and castigating the other political parties that he considered "dangerous. He said: "I am a nationalist, I want Quebec to be more autonomous, with more power, and there are three parties, the Green Party, the Liberal Party and the NDP, who are asking for less autonomy." If he had it to do over again, Quebec Premier François Legault wanted the minority Conservatives elected because they felt that the CPC was far less centralizing than the other parties and that the demands he made in his letter would be listened to more carefully by Erin O'Toole.

There were many reactions in the sovereignist camp and among many members of the Bloc Québécois. The former leader of *Québec Solidaire*, Françoise David, was highly critical of Legault's intervention, pointing out that voters could decide for themselves and that the Conservative Party is light years away from the values of Quebecers. We need only think of the issues related to climate change or gun control (David 2021). On election night and in light of the election results, François Legault still maintained that his decision was the right one: "I don't regret having defended the autonomy of the Quebec nation, I will continue to do so throughout my mandate", the Premier assured (Martel 2021).

THE RETURN OF IDENTITY ISSUES: THE TELEVISED DEBATE IN ENGLISH

The end of the election campaign was marked by a particular event that took place during the televised debate in English. The moderator of the debate, Shachi Kurl, began by asking Yves-François Blanchet why his party was defending the Legault government's Secularism Act and Bill 96 on the French language while claiming that there was no problem of racism in Quebec (Vastel 2021). The question was clearly biased and drew strong reactions from Quebec and Canadian political elites. More problematic was the fact that the producer of the debate responsible for the editorial issues was a media group that included APTN, CBC, CTV and Global on the English side. According to its spokesperson, the "official English debate editorial board", composed of production managers, producers and journalists from the four media outlets, had validated the issue and continued to justify the relevance of Shachi Kurl's intervention (Proulx 2021a, b). Moreover, Shachi Kurl wrote that she had no regrets, she was not going to apologize and she stands by what she said (Kurl 2021). However, the host's attitude was a clear example of the strong anti-Quebec sentiment that exists in various parts of Canada (Labelle 2021).

Even if voting intentions for the Bloc Québécois did not really move in the last month of the campaign, the effect was undoubtedly that Bloc voters weighed a little more heavily on the pencil in the ballot box while making them immune to the other political parties. This is essentially what journalist Konrad Yakabuski said when he wrote: "Had it not been for this turn of events, the Bloc would certainly have lost several ridings in the greater Montreal area on Monday night. Although Mr. Blanchet's position as party leader is not threatened, the future of the Bloc appears uncertain. A party that relies mostly on Quebec in the rest of Canada to mobilize its voters is never far from its expiration date" (Yakabuski 2021) (Fig. 5.3).

It should also be mentioned that the turn of the debate also put a grain of salt in the strategy of the Quebec government, undermining in some ways its willingness to get closer to the Conservative Party of Erin O'Toole. In addition, the Conservative leader as well as Justin Trudeau did not intervene during this exchange, understanding such an intervention could harm their campaign in Quebec. The two leaders wanted to calm the game by stating after the debate that "Quebecers are not racist".

The debate has thus reopened the debate on the identity proposals of the Bloc Québécois program. Quebecers form a nation, a proud people, proud of their history, a North American civilization. Those who constantly seek to denigrate this unique and original culture that seeks to

INTENTIONS DE VOTE AU QUÉBEC

CP1A et B. Si des élections FÉDÉRALES avaient lieu aujourd'hui, pour quel parti auriez-vous l'intention de voter? Est-ce que ce serait pour...
Dans le cas où un-e répondant-e était sans opinion, la question de relance suivante était posée : Même si votre choix n'est pas encore fait, pour lequel des partis politiques suivants auriez-vous le plus tendance à voter? Serait-ce pour... Si vous avez déjà voté par anticipation, veuillez indiquer pour lequel des partis vous avez voté.
Base: Les répondant-e-s du Québec (n=925). Le Bloc Québécois était affiché uniquement aux répondant-e-s du Québec et le Parti Maverick était affiché uniquement aux répondant-e-s de l'Alberta et du Manitoba.

	Québec	Langue Franco	Langue Non Franco
n pondéré =	455	351	103
n absolu =	925	755	169
... le Parti libéral du Canada, de Justin Trudeau	33%	28%	48%
... le Bloc Québécois, d'Yves-François Blanchet	32%	38%	10%
... le Parti conservateur du Canada, d'Erin O'Toole	19%	19%	17%
... le Nouveau Parti démocratique du Canada, de Jagmeet Singh	11%	10%	17%
... le Parti populaire du Canada, de Maxime Bernier	4%	3%	5%
... le Parti vert du Canada, d'Annamie Paul	1%	1%	2%
... le Parti Maverick, de Jay Hill	-	-	-
...un autre parti	0%	1%	0%

Fig. 5.3 Voting intention in Québec—September 14–17, 2021 (*Source* https://legermarketing.wpenginepowered.com/wp-content/uploads/2021/09/Rapport-politique-federale-18-sept-2021_VFinale-media.pdf)

survive in its language through its institutions and its worthy representatives inevitably hit a wall. Sacha Kurl's question raises a fundamental issue. What is the place of Quebec in this country that many Quebecers feel they have built since the time when Quebec was the capital of Canada? The deep resentment of English Canadians towards the co-founders of the country only brings back to the forefront an existential question: What are we doing in a country that is more and more foreign to Quebecers and that systematically refuses to recognize one of the most living cultures of this country? The role of the Bloc in Ottawa is to remind the Canadian elites of the essence of Quebec values and that it is ready to negotiate with the other provinces its exit from the Canadian fold, which is sovereignty-association. This is undoubtedly why the Bloc is a good example of a niche party in its ability to bring to the electoral market issues that its opponents do not wish to address, but which reach its electorate.

Conclusion

The Bloc Québécois would certainly have liked to have elected 40 MPs, which would no doubt have enabled it to be more influential in the House of Commons against the Liberal government and Justin Trudeau. For François Legault, such a majority of seats would have allowed him to have a group of parliamentarians in Ottawa ready to explain to the rest of Canada the reasons for his political choices. When the Bloc was created more than thirty years ago, its raison d'être was certainly strategic, especially in a pre-referendum context. Over the years, this party has evolved, transformed itself and then experienced internal crises to become a real niche party: that of representing the interests of the citizens of Quebec and secondarily that of the party in power in Quebec. A comparative analysis of the electoral platforms of federal political parties that considers the absence or presence of proposals directly affecting Quebec voters, could be interesting in order to demonstrate the importance of having a unique voice for Quebec in Ottawa.

In any political campaign, mistakes are to be expected from parties, leaders and candidates. This was the case for Yves-François Blanchet on the third link and for the leader of the CAQ with his support for the Conservative Party. But the prize goes to the host of the English language debate, who gave ammunition to the Bloc camp by making herself the spokesperson for a certain kind of Quebec-bashing, much to the chagrin of the other federal parties. Identity issues are certainly at the heart of a niche party such as the Bloc Québécois, which to some extent favoured a certain popular comeback at the end of the campaign. There is no doubt that the debate in English was a turning point in the campaign.

Strategically, Quebec voters understood that by favouring the election of Bloc Québécois MPs, the chances of having a minority government in Ottawa, whether Liberal or Conservative, was more than likely. This was the analysis of Brian Myles, editor of Le Devoir, two days before the election, without endorsing the BQ: "The Bloc has always played a constructive role in the Commons. It has contributed to the progress of the work and to its enrichment by its attachment to the Quebec perspective. There is no ambiguity in the Bloc's discourse on the defence of the French fact and the Quebec nation. Its members will stand up every day to remind the self-righteous English Canadian elites of Quebec's prerogatives in asserting its language, its culture and its distinct institutions. This voice is needed in the current climate to consolidate and expand Quebec's autonomy within the federation" (Myles 2021).

Clearly, the 2021 federal election will have demonstrated that a party like the Bloc Québécois not only has a raison d'être, but that it is useful in defending the views of many voters, and that it represents the aspirations of many voters. According to the last poll of the election campaign, the Bloc received the support of 38% of francophone voters, compared to 25% for the Liberal Party of Canada. If the issue of Quebec's national status was left unaddressed in the 2021 federal election, one can legitimately wonder what the issues will be in the next federal election!

References

Tarik Abouo-Chadi, "Niche Party Success and Mainstream Party Policy Shifts—How Green and Radical Right Parties Differ in Their Impact", *British Journal of Political Science*, 46 (2), April 2016: 417–436.

Marco Bélair-Cirino, "L'ère des demi-victoires - Les gouvernements minoritaires fréquents à Ottawa depuis 20 ans, mais sont-ils devenus la règle?", *Le Devoir*, September 25–26, 2021, B-2 and B-3.

Bloc Québécois, *Bloc Québécois, Plateforme politique—Bloc 2021*, August 2021. https://www.blocquebecois.org/plateforme/.

André Bouthillier, *Le goût du risque - Récit d'un parcours professionnel exaltant*, Montréal, Somme Toute/Le Devoir, 2022.

Patrick Butler and Neil Collins, "Strategic Analysis in Political Markets", *European Journal of Marketing*, 30 (10/11), 1996: 25–36.

Marie-France Charbonneau and Guy Lachapelle, *Le Bloc Québécois: 20 ans au nom du Québec*, Richard Vézina éditeur, 2010.

Mylène Crête, "Élections fédérales - 38 promesses pour contrer une majorité libérale", *Le Devoir*, August 23, 2021, pp. A1 and A4.

M. N. Clemente, *The Marketing Glossary*, New York: Amacon, 1992.

Francoise David, "Une intervention troublante", *La Presse*, September 11, 2021.

Sébastien Desrosiers, "Le Bloc Québécois tire sur tout ce qui est rouge", *Radio-Canada*, August 22, 2021.

Government du Québec, "Federal Election—Premier François Legault Asks Federal Party Leaders for Firm Commitments on Health and Immigration", Office of the Premier, 26 August 2021.

Susan Harada and Helen Morris, "Niche Marketing the Greens in Canada and Scotland", in Jennifer Lees-Marshment, *Routledge Handbook of Political Marketing*, Routledge, 2012.

Ronald Inglehart, *Culture Shift in Advanced Industrial Society*, Princeton, NJ, Princeton University Press, 1990.

Dave King, 2021, "Caroline Keeps Her Seat", *Le Charlevoisien*, 26 (34), September 22, 2021: 3.

Shachi Kurl, "I Was Asked to Apologize for My Question in the Leaders' Debate. I Stand by It Unequivocally", *The Globe and Mail*, September 25, 2021. https://www.theglobeandmail.com/amp/opinion/article-i-was-asked-to-apologize-for-my-question-in-the-leaders-debate-i-stand/.

Micheline Labelle, "Le Quebec bashing, un acharnement persistant et sans retenue", *Le Devoir*, September 18–19, 2021, B-12.

Étienne Lajoie, "Une "francophobie" émerge à l'Université d'Ottawa", *Le Devoir*, October 2, 2021.

Jean-François Lisée, "Le Bloc et le nœud gordien", *Le Devoir*, September 18–19, 2021, B-12.

Philippe J. Maarek, *Campaign Communication & Political Marketing*, Wiley-Blackwell, 2011.

Éric Martel, "François Legault Does Not Regret His Support for the Conservatives", *Métro*, 21 September 2021.

BM Meguid, "Competition Between Unequals: The Role of Mainstream Party Strategy in Niche Party Success", *American Political Science Review* 99, 2005: 347–359.

Thomas M. Meyer and Bernhard Miller, "The Niche Party Concept and Its Measurement", *Party Politics*, 21 (2), 2015: 259–271.

Éric Montigny, "The Bloc Québécois as a Safe Bet", in Jon H. Pammet and Christopher Dornan (eds.), *The 2021 Canadian Federal Election*, Montreal, McGill-Queen's University Press, 2022, 84–104.

Bryan Myles, "Tout ça pour ça?", *Le Devoir*, September 18–19, 2021, B10.

Winther Nielsen, "Three Faces of Political Marketing Strategy", *Journal of Public Affairs*, 12 (4), 2012: 293–302.

Henri Ouellette-Vézina, "Triggering the Federal Election—'We're Playing a Bit of Russian Roulette'", *La Presse*, August 14, 2021. https://www.lapresse.ca/actualites/politique/2021-08-14/declenchement-de-l-election-federale/on-joue-un-peu-a-la-roulette-russe.php.

Caroline Plante, "Blanchet favorable à un troisième lien entre Québec et Lévis", *Le Devoir*, August 25, 2021, A-4.

Boris Proulx, "Élections fédérales - L'animatrice du débat des chefs en anglais défend sa question controversée", *Le Devoir*, September 11, 2021.

Boris Proulx, "Les écologistes consternés par la position du Bloc sur le troisième lien", *Le Devoir*, August 26, 2021, A-5.

Anne-Marie Provost, "La bataille des banlieues", *Le Devoir*, September 15, 2021, A1 and A8.

Alexandre Sirois, "Triggering the Federal Election—Trudeau and the Burden of Proof", *La Presse*, August 14, 2021.

Naël Shiab, "Results: Here's Where the Election Was Played Out in Maps", *Radio-Canada*, October 22, 2019. https://ici.radio-canada.ca/info/2019/elections-federales/resultats-cartes-vainqueur-perdant-partis-circonscriptions/.

Rosanna Tiranti, "Legault Supports the Conservatives", *Journal Métro*, September 2021.

Union des producteurs agricoles, *Regional Profile of the Biofood Industry in Quebec*, 2015.

Marie Vastel, "Legault, le perdant du débat des chefs en anglais?", *Le Devoir*, September 11, 2021.

Konrad Yakabuski, "Chefs en sursis", *Le Devoir*, September 25–26, 2021, B-12.

CHAPTER 6

The People's Party of Canada and the Appeal of Anger Politics

André Turcotte, David Coletto, and Simon Vodrey

Abstract In the 2021 Canadian federal election, the People's Party of Canada (PPC), a marginal, poorly organized, and badly funded party managed to get 5% of the popular vote with a rancorous and divisive discourse. Drawing on extensive opinion polling conducted during the election campaign, we isolate and define the appeal of anger politics in the most recent Canadian election. We point out that Maxime Bernier's party

---

The original version of this chapter was revised: Misspelled author name has been corrected. The correction to this chapter is available at
https://doi.org/10.1007/978-3-031-34404-6_10

A. Turcotte (✉) · S. Vodrey
School of Journalism and Communication, Carleton University, Ottawa, ON, Canada
e-mail: andre.turcotte@carleton.ca

D. Coletto
Abacus Data, Ottawa, ON, Canada
e-mail: david@abacusdata.ca

© The Author(s), under exclusive license to Springer Nature Switzerland AG 2023, corrected publication 2023
J. Gillies et al. (eds.), *Political Marketing in the 2021 Canadian Federal Election*, Palgrave Studies in Political Marketing and Management,
https://doi.org/10.1007/978-3-031-34404-6_6

is the latest manifestation in a long tradition in federal politics; fuelled by economic and social grievances and galvanized by charismatic leadership. We show that while the PPC failed to win a seat during the election, it demonstrated that anger remains a mobilizing electoral force for some Canadian voters. Moreover, with an economic recession looming and the precariousness of a minority government, it is likely that "anger" will persist as part of the current electoral calculus in Canada.

Keywords People's Party · Populism · Grievances · Anger · COVID-19

On the surface, the 2021 Canadian federal election was largely uneventful. After thirty-six days of campaigning, the governing Liberals were re-elected winning five more seats than in 2019 but were once again denied a majority in the House of Commons. Both the second-place Conservatives and third-place Bloc Québécois won the exact same number of seats they had at the start of the campaign. The election appeared so uneventful that pundits began to refer to it as the *Seinfeld* election—an election where nothing really happened. But this description is more a reflection of the outcome than the campaign itself. Many un-Canadian things happened during the campaign. For instance, there was an unusually high level of vitriolic discourse and protests. Canadians even witnessed their Prime Minister being pelted by protesters on the campaign trail. The outcome was devastating for two party leaders. Green Party Leader Annamie Paul resigned two months after the election and Conservative Leader Erin O'Toole was ousted a few months later.

Also lost amidst the apparent monotony of the campaign was the performance of the troops led by Maxime Bernier. The People's Party of Canada (PPC), a marginal, poorly organized, and badly funded party managed to get 5% of the popular vote with a rancorous and divisive discourse. The PPC failed to win a seat during the election but demonstrated that anger was a mobilizing electoral force for some Canadian voters. The PPC may have failed to win seats but within a year, more angry manifestations littered the Canadian political landscape, from a Freedom Convoy occupying the nation's capital to a surprising showing by another marginal political party in a provincial election in Québec. Then came the selection of Danielle Smith as leader of the United Conservative Party (UCP) and Premier of Alberta.

This chapter examines the appeal of the PPC in the 2021 Canadian federal election. We analyze who supported the PPC and what were their main motivations for doing so, with a special look at the role of anger in their voting calculus. Protest movements are nothing new in Canada and in many ways, the PPC is just the latest incarnation. However, subsequent events suggest that this party successfully tapped into public sentiment—however marginal—and may be indicative of a phenomenon larger than its negligible electoral performance. Drawing from literature going back to Neil Nevitte's *The Decline of Deference: Canadian Value Change in Cross-National Perspective* (1996), more recent works on *"anger"* as a motivating factor in politics (see for instance Mishra 2017; Cramer 2016; Engels 2015), and extensive opinion polling conducted during the election campaign, we will isolate and define the appeal of anger politics. While our starting point is PPC supporters, we intend to draw some extension between the 2021 Canadian federal election and more recent events in Canada and abroad.

Protest and Anger in Politics: A Review

The use of protest and anger as motivating or mobilizing factors in politics is anything but a recent development. As long as the art of politics has been practised, both have been significant motivators for certain voters. But as the proportion of those voters for which protest and anger are motivating factors, either through the act of voting itself or the act of physical protesting, in Canada and elsewhere increased in the recent past—and, if so, why? This is a key question with which our chapter grapples. Yet before we can address that question, we need to review the historical and theoretical context in which protest and anger in politics have ebbed and flowed.

Andrew Linklater (2022) addresses this topic by explaining that Hugo Grotius, the renowned Dutch diplomat, lawyer, poet, playwright, theologian, and Renaissance Man (both literally and figuratively), offered an early interpretation of the role of anger in the seventeenth century when he reasoned that "anger is a destructive force that must be held in check by 'higher' emotions such as compassion" (575). That said, according to Linklater, "anger has not always been presented in that light". Attitudes to the emotion were far more ambivalent in "warrior societies" and in "classical antiquity" (575). Anger, resentment, and retribution were considered to be more commonplace and acceptable motivating factors in the politics of the "pre-modern era" (i.e., the pre-Enlightenment Era) than in its aftermath (Althoff 1998; Jaeger 1985; Linklater 2022).

Of course, the anger, resentment, and retribution in the pre-modern era were often expressed differently than in the centuries that followed.

For instance, in the politics of the pre-modern era, they were typically expressed physically through acts of violence which we consider as "hot anger". In contrast, "cold anger", is expressed not through physical violence but through non-violent forms of political participation, such as participating in a political protest. "Cold anger" could also be expressed by disassociating from those who hold opposing political perspectives and ideologies in interpersonal relationships, or by voting for a certain candidate not because of the candidate's platform but because of the belief that voting a certain way is a form of expressing anger, resentment, and retribution against another political candidate or apparatus. To take a step back then, we apply the distinction between hot anger and cold anger that Federica Biassoni et al. (2016) made in vocal and acoustic studies to the political realm. For instance, they reason that "Although hot anger corresponds to the prototypical full-blown anger emotion, milder and more subtle forms of anger expression exist and are generally known as *cold anger* (e.g., irritation)" (2). Channelling the work of Tanja Banzinger and Klaus Scherer (2005) as well as Petri Laukka et al. (2011), they elaborate that, "these less intense forms of emotional expressions are more frequently occurring in everyday life [...and] compared with hot anger, cold anger is thought to be less intense and characterized by lower levels of arousal" (Biassoni et al. 2016, p. 2). And, in the political realm, Linklater (2022) sums the matter up for us: "The ethic of self-restraint [...] sought to replace anger with mercy and moderation" (576). However, has that replacement truly occurred?

We argue that, while anger may no longer be acceptably expressed through violence in politics, it is commonly expressed in contemporary politics through non-violent means and these non-violent means are becoming increasingly commonplace in North American politics. If this is so, it is also important to remember, as Katherine J. Cramer (2016) reminds us, that, "The seeds of resentment are sown over long periods of time" (19). Those seeds need to be carefully cultivated and they do not sprout quickly. The fact that elections in both Canada and the United States are increasingly being won on ever smaller margins than in decades past tends to amplify the importance of tribal marketing, wedge politics, and identity politics—all of which are aimed less at persuading voters and more at mobilizing voters who are already aligned with a particular ideological perspective, a particular party, or a particular candidate (Cramer 2016; Fukuyama 2018; McQuarrie 2017; Webster et al. 2022). Related to this is the increasingly important subject of polarization in Canadian and American politics.

To put it simply, both Americans and Canadians have become progressively polarized over the past few decades (Cramer 2016; Fukuyama 2018; Veroni 2014; Webster et al. 2022). Steven W. Webster, Elizabeth C. Connors and Betsy Sinclair (2022) shine a light on this accelerating political polarization and why it is problematic by explaining that "A functioning democracy relies on social interactions between people who disagree — including listening to others' viewpoints, having political discussions, and finding political compromise" (1292). Unfortunately, interactions such as those are happening less frequently than in the past (Cramer 2016; Fukuyama 2018; Webster et al. 2022). Furthermore, despite their importance to the proper working of the democratic process, contemporary political discussion networks are rarely heterogenous. In fact, those on opposing political sides are unlikely to even have friendly social interactions, let alone fruitful political discussions, with each other (1292). To make matters worse, people are increasingly avoiding any interaction with anyone who does not hold the same political beliefs as themselves (Cramer 2016; Fukuyama 2018). This active avoidance of contrasting opinions is particularly problematic because, "its effects extend beyond the political arena" (Webster et al. 2022, 1293). In other words, who one socializes with, who one forms relationships with, who one works with, who one lives with and, in extreme circumstances, who one is even willing to cordially converse with, is increasingly becoming limited to those who hold the same political and ideological perspectives and opinions (Cramer 2016; Fukuyama 2018; Webster et al. 2022). Sadly, when conversing with an individual who holds a different political and ideological perspective, as Katherine J. Cramer (2016) reveals, the following type of response is becoming more commonplace: "'I don't talk to people like you'" (3).

In essence, political polarization is becoming increasingly common, and increasingly corrosive, and is seeping into many more areas of North American life than just those associated with political contestation (Cramer 2016; Hochschild 2018; Resnick 2000; Veroni 2014; Webster 2020). Along with this is what Cramer (2016) and others (Engels 2015; Fukuyama 2018; Resnick 2000; Wuthnow 2019) have referred to as a "politics of resentment." Some of its key attributes include the following:

A politics of resentment arises from the way social identities, the emotion of resentment, and economic insecurity interact. In a politics of resentment, resentment toward fellow citizens is front and center. People understand their circumstances as the fault of guilty and less deserving social groups, not as the product of broad social, economic, and political forces. (9)

Put differently, a politics of resentment is increasingly visceral, increasingly localized, and increasingly commonplace. More aspects of life that were not previously considered grounds for political contestation are now being seen as just that: the kind of car one drives; the kind of sports practised and hobbies enjoyed; the kind of stores frequented are just a few such new battlegrounds of political contestation (Cramer 2016; Engels 2015; Fukuyama 2018; Resnick 2000; Veroni 2014; Webster 2020; Webster et al. 2022; Wuthnow 2019).

Geography also plays an important role in accounting for whether or not protest and anger act as motivating and mobilizing factors in politics (Cramer 2016; Hochschild 2018; McQuarrie 2017; Resnick 2000; Wuthnow 2019). As Michael McQuarrie (2017) succinctly puts it: "Regional particularity matters" (S146). He elaborates on this statement by arguing that "the articulation in geography cannot be explained without a consideration of the dynamics of place" (S125). In essence, geographic regions are not interchangeable. Whether it be for differences of opinion on resource extraction and energy consumption, differences of opinion on notions of sovereignty, differences of opinion on the role of the federal government's intervention on matters of health care or education (to name but a few), geography plays an increasingly important role in relations to political anger (Cramer 2016; Hochschild 2018; McQuarrie 2017; Resnick 2000; Wuthnow 2019). Over the past few electoral cycles, both in Canada and the United States, one of the most significant factors contributing to polarization is the increasing ideological gulf between rural and urban voters (Cramer 2016; Hochschild 2018; McQuarrie 2017; Wuthnow 2019). With this in mind, Cramer (2016) identifies that throughout much of America, many of those living outside of populated urban centers express a "rural consciousness" and that a fundamental component of rural consciousness is that, "an identity as a rural person [...] includes much more than an attachment to place" (5). It is more complicated than that. For instance, it includes a sense that decision-makers routinely ignore rural places and fail to give rural communities their fair share of resources, as well as a sense that rural folks are fundamentally different from urbanites in terms of lifestyles, values, and work ethic. Rural consciousness signals an identification with rural people and rural places and denotes multifaceted resentment against cities (5–6). To be fair, this is not a purely American phenomenon. The same ideological gulf is present here in Canada as well (Nevitte 1996; Resnick 2000; Veroni 2014). Canada is more than just Toronto, Montreal, Ottawa, and Vancouver. Yet for decades, the political priorities of countless federal governments of all stripes as well as the mainstream media's coverage of those priorities would have many believe otherwise.

For their part, Webster et al. (2022) inject another important caveat into the discussion held thus far about the role of anger, resentment, and retribution as motivations in the current North American political environment when they argue that despite the secular increase in anger among the mass public [...,] it is clear that this increase has not been monotonic. On the contrary, in some electoral cycles [...] anger appears to be a particularly salient feature of political competition. In other years [...] mass-level anger is less pronounced. (1295) If we are weighing the salience of anger as a motivator in American politics, the two most recent U.S. presidential elections quickly come to mind as vivid examples. But, to take a step back from discussions of political polarization and geography, we must ask an important question: what societal forces are contributing to these changes? Neil Nevitte (1996) helps illuminate a key such force in the very aptly named title of his work: *The Decline of Deference: Canadian Value Change in Cross-National Perspective*. Even though it has been nearly thirty years since Nevitte's analysis was published, his key findings are still relevant in assessing contemporary Canadian politics. For example, his identification of "the erosion of institutional authority, and the rise of citizen intervention in politics" are more pronounced today than ever could have been imagined in the mid-1990s (5). Furthermore, as he notes, while reflecting upon the period of 1981–1990:

> Citizen confidence in a whole array of governmental institutions (parliaments and civilian bureaucracies of one sort or another) dwindled, as did confidence in a variety of non-governmental institutions such as the education system, the media, and churches. At the same time, people became more inclined to approve of protest types of political behaviour, and support for a variety of social movements increased. Politics became more boisterous and citizens more cranky. (288)

With the proliferation of cable TV news, the advent of the Internet and its tendency to stoke the fires of conspiracy theorists and to galvanize ideological echo chambers just as much as it allows free-wheeling access to diverse opinions and "objective" information—not to mention contested elections, and a once-in-a-century global pandemic, all occurring after 1990—politics is not surprisingly substantially "more boisterous and citizens more cranky" than they were at the time of Nevitte's writing (288). Nevitte (1996), sums up why such a decline of deference characterized by increasingly "cranky" and "boisterous" voters and citizens likely occurred when he explains that, "Canadian values may have changed partly because of the structural and value shifts associated with late industrialism, partly because of proximity to the United States, and partly because of the kinds of orientations that new Canadians contribute" (p. 18). The first (late industrialism) and third (immigration patterns) of these can certainly be witnessed below the 49th Parallel and across much of the United States as well (Fukuyama 2018; Mishra 2017).

In other words, values are not held constant: they shift over time and are also subject to influence from outside forces as Nevitte (1996) posits. And, in his eyes, scholars should pay careful attention to mapping the shifts of values over time since, "Values, or deep dispositions, are important because they guide decisions about right and wrong and because they underpin a whole array of social, economic, and political preferences" (p. 19). In addition to this important point, Nevitte channels the work of Milton Rokeach (1968) when he argues that values are also important considerations when weighing the contemporary trajectory of protest and anger as motivating factors in American and Canadian politics because values "are foundations for action, foundations that help to explain regularities, or indeed irregularities, in people's behaviour" (Nevitte 1996, 19). It is important to remember that values—fixed or fluid—are often associated with conceptions of identity (Cramer 2016; Fukuyama 2018; McQuarrie 2017; Mishra 2017; Nevitte 1996; Veroni 2014). According to Francis Fukuyama (2018):

> The modern concept of identity unites three different phenomena. The first is thymos, a universal aspect of human personality that craves recognition. The second is the distinction between the inner and the outer self, and the raising of the moral valuation of the inner self over outer society [...] The third is an evolving concept of dignity, in which recognition is due not just to a narrow class of people, but to everyone. (37)

With these three building blocks of identity in mind, the current omnipresence of identity politics in the North American political landscape appears to be a logical if not inevitable outcome. As Fukuyama puts it himself: "We cannot get away from identity or identity politics" (163). Identity politics is so pervasive because, "societies divide themselves into smaller and smaller groups by virtue of their particular 'lived experience' of victimization" (p. 164). In a similar vein to Nevitte (1996), Fukuyama (2018) maintains that "Confusion over identity arises as a condition of living in the modern world. Modernization means constant change and disruption, and the opening up of choices that did not exist before" (164).

Adding another voice to this topic, Pankaj Mishra (2017) argues that advanced capitalism and advanced technologies have played a substantial role in promoting resentment. In his eyes, "individuals with very different pasts find themselves herded by capitalism and technology into a common present, where grossly unequal distributions of wealth and power have created humiliating new hierarchies" (13). And this "common present" breeds resentment (13). It does so through a process of coveting spurred by mediated comparisons (13). As Mishra explains, "This proximity, or what Hannah Arendt called 'negative solidarity', is rendered more claustrophobic by digital communications, the improved capacity for envious and resentful comparison, and the commonplace, and therefore compromised, quest for individual distinction and singularity" (13). To make matters worse, according to Mishra,

> The result is, as [Hannah] Arendt feared, a 'tremendous increase in mutual hatred and a somewhat universal irritability of everybody against everybody else,' or ressentiment. An existential resentment of other people's being, caused by an intense mix of envy and sense of humiliation and powerlessness, ressentiment, as it lingers and deepens, poisons civil society and undermines political liberty. (14)

In other words, resentment can fester until it turns into ressentiment and these two corrosive forces—the latter of which is more corrosive than the former—are increasingly seeping into the North American political landscape. For better or for worse, the proliferation of anger and protest as motivating and mobilizing factors in politics can be seen as natural by-products of this process.

Returning to Webster, Connors, and Sinclair (2022) allows us to transition to putting the People's Party of Canada in context and then to more acutely and granularly analyse the appeal of anger and protest politics in contemporary Canadian politics at large. To those ends, they remind us that "Anger, then, is an emotion that is commonly expressed by the mass public. However, the public is neither perpetually nor uniformly angry. On the contrary, the degree to which [they] express political anger varies across electoral cycles" (p. 1295). Furthermore, "This variation occurs — at least partially — due to differences in elites' attempts to arouse their base and citizens' attentiveness to such appeals" (1295).

THE PEOPLE'S PARTY IN CONTEXT

Maxime Bernier was angry, and some would say, for good reasons. On May 27, 2017, on the 13th round of voting and after leading in all the previous twelve rounds, Bernier lost the Conservative leadership vote to Andrew Scheer by a mere 1.9 percentage points. Immediately, Bernier cried foul play and criticized the voting process. About one year later, Bernier left the Conservative Party and went on to set up *"The People's Party of Canada"* on September 14, 2018. The Party ran in 2019 on a platform *against* political correctness, immigration, and climate change. The party platform would add *Covid-19 restrictions* and *vaccine mandates* to its platform ahead of the 2021 federal election. The People's Party is not the first nor likely the last protest party in Canada. At different moments in time, several politicians attempted to ride the people's anger to 24 Sussex Drive and while all fell short—at least at the federal level—some were more successful than others. It is beyond the scope of this section to review all the different and disparate protest parties in Canada since there are too numerous to count. The focus will be limited to the federal scene and those efforts which may have something in common with *The People's Party of Canada*.

The first federal political formation to overtly tap into voters' anger—and arguably the most successful electorally—was the Progressive Party. Born out of the adversity of the First World War, the party elected 65 MPs on a platform against what they saw as preferential treatment for "eastern manufacturers, bankers, and other elite groups at the expense of ordinary producers" (LeDuc et al. 2016: 114). They emerged as the second-largest party in Parliament but refused to act as a coherent official opposition and quickly disappeared. The 1935 federal election was another early catalyst for the emergence of parties born out of anger. At that time, the country was reeling from the aftermath of the Great Depression and some voters found solace in protest. One such formation was the Reconstruction Party founded by former Liberal MP H.H. Stevens. Stevens left the Liberal Party in protest of how Mackenzie King handled his recommendations from the Royal Commission he chaired. The Commission put forth proposals to fight profiteering against consumers and King largely ignored them (LeDuc et al. 2016). Stevens managed to win his seat, but the Reconstruction Party quickly faded away. Two other new political formations ran candidates in the 1935 election. The Social Credit—already in power provincially in Alberta under the leadership of the popular "Bible Bill" Aberhart—ran on a protest platform directed against the financial system. At the other end of the spectrum, the Cooperative Commonwealth Federation (CCF) also ran candidates in 1935 protesting the neglect towards low-income and rural Canadians. The CCF eventually morphed into the New Democratic Party (NDP) and remains an important force in Canadian politics.

We encounter Social Credit again in the 1960s. More precisely, *Les Créditistes*, the Quebec-wing of the Social Credit. This party is interesting for our discussion because it had a lot of the key elements of an impactful protest party. The Quebec Leader, Réal Caouette, was very charismatic and understood how to tap into Quebec's anger. With a Diefenbaker government that was either dismissive or hostile towards Quebec and the appearance that the Liberal Party was turning towards the intellectual and urban elites for support, Caouette relentlessly campaigned in rural Quebec and "spread the message that Quebec had nothing to lose in voting for Social Credit" (Leduc et al. 2016: 217). This proved to be an appealing message for *Les Créditistes* who managed to win 26 Quebec seats in 1962, 27 in 1963 and 18 in 1965.

While previous protest parties emerged from grievances born out of economic disparities and inequalities, the most recent iterations were the results of anger towards regional inequalities and constitutional wrangling. When the Mulroney government awarded a lucrative aircraft maintenance contract to Quebec-based Bombardier over better offers from Western provinces especially Manitoba, Preston Manning cried foul, decried the blatant catering to Quebec and established the Reform Party of Canada. The 1992 Referendum, during which Manning cleverly encouraged Canadians to "Know More" about the proposed Charlottetown Accord further fueled regional and constitutional resentment.

This led to the devastating PC defeat in 1993 and eventually the rise of Reform to Official Opposition status. After some years of middling performance, Manning gambled to try to "Unite the Right" which led to the creation of the Canadian Alliance. Anger towards the performance of the new leader Stockwell Day resulted in the splintering of this party and the creation of yet another short-lived political formation; the Democratic Representative Caucus (DRC) under the joint leadership of Chuck Strahl and Joe Clark. Eventually, all those parties coalesced into the new Conservative Party of Canada. This constitutional turmoil also led to the making of the Bloc Québécois. As noted in *Dynasties and Interludes* (2010): "moderate nationalists in Quebec, who had once gravitated to Mulroney as a native son, became either radicalized or marginalized politically following the demise of the Meech Lake Accord and the failure of the Charlottetown referendum" (413) They united under another favorite son, Lucien Bouchard, who had bolted from the Mulroney Cabinet. The Bloc became the Official Opposition in 1993 and remains an important force on the federal scene.

A few lessons can be learned from the aforementioned one hundred years of anger politics in Canada. First, protest parties tend to emerge out of hardship—mostly but not limited to economic hardship. The parties give voice to those affected and provide electoral order to their anger. Second, somewhere along the way, some real or imaginary slights are perceived which act as a catalyst to the formation of a new political party. Third, it appears that internal discord and infighting are important factors in explaining the emergence of protest movements. And finally, charismatic leadership is often involved. In greatly varied ways, Stevens, Caouette, Manning, and Bouchard were able to connect with disenfranchised voters and successfully tap into their anger. Our analysis examines the extent to which these factors also contribute to explaining the People's Party.

Analysis

To assess the profile and opinions of those who supported the *People's Party of Canada* during the 2021 Canadian election, we used survey data collected by Abacus Data over five waves in the lead-up and during the 2021 Canadian election. A total of 13,931 interviews were conducted from a nationally representative online survey from September 9 to October 19, 2021. This sample included 304 respondents who indicated they would vote for the *People's Party of Canada*. In the Abacus Data surveys, some 5% of respondents said they would vote for the *People's Party of Canada*, an estimate almost exact to the party's actual performance in the election. First, we profile who voted for the *People's Party of Canada* and how they differ from other electors. Then we test our hypotheses by looking at what *People's Party of Canada* supporters think and how their views compared with others in the electorate.

Profiling People's Party of Canada Supporting

People's Party of Canada voters tended to be younger, male, and more likely to report being unemployed than other electors during the 2021 Canadian election. Some 55% were under 44 years of age, compared with 44% of the rest of the electorate. Similarly, 64% were male compared with 49% of the rest of the electorate. Accordingly, about 1 in 3 *People's Party of Canada* supporters were male and under the age of 44.

People's Party of Canada supporters are as likely to self-identify from a racialized community as other electors but are less likely to be born outside of Canada than other electorates. About 17% of PPC supporters are from a racialized community compared with 20% of other electors. Moreover, 9% are born outside of Canada compared with 19% of other electors.

The household income distribution of *People's Party of Canada* supporters is like the rest of the electorate. They are not more likely to come from different income groups. However, there is a significant education gap. Despite being much younger than the electorate as a whole, *People's Party of Canada* supporters are less likely to have a university degree than the rest of the electorate (23% vs. 32%) and are far more likely to be childless than the rest of the electorate (63% vs. 49%). Although 8% of working-age electors reported being unemployed, 31% of *People's Party of Canada* supporters said they were unemployed.

Compared with other electors, *People's Party of Canada* supporters were primarily male, younger, and more likely to be economically displaced. They were more likely to be born in Canada but as likely to self-identify as a member of a racialized community. *People's Party of Canada* supporters are not just demographically and economically different from other electors, they also hold very different opinions and attitudes. What differentiates them more than anything else is their outlook on the country's political system and their views on the COVID-19 pandemic, vaccinations, and Canadian Prime Minister Justin Trudeau.

WHAT PEOPLE'S PARTY OF CANADA SUPPORTERS THINK

As expected, *People's Party of Canada* supporters were deeply dissatisfied with the direction of the country and of its political leadership. Only 15% thought at the time that Canada was headed in the right direction, twenty-three percentage points less likely than other electors. At the same time, *People's Party of Canada* supporters were more pessimistic about the future with 51% disagreeing that they are very optimistic about the future compared with 32% of other electors.

People's Party of Canada supporters were also deeply unhappy with Canada's Prime Minister. 75% reported having a very negative impression of Prime Minister Justin Trudeau during the election. This intense dislike for Prime Minister Trudeau was substantially higher than the rest of the electorate—including supporters of other opposition parties. Among other electors, 27% had a very negative view of Prime Minister Trudeau.

These two factors—a deep dislike for the Prime Minister and leader of the Liberal Party and a general dissatisfaction with the direction of the country were largely a factor of how *People's Party of Canada* supporters felt about the COVID-19 pandemic, vaccine mandates, and the approach the Canadian government took in response to the pandemic overall.

What unites *People's Party of Canada* the most is their opposition to COVID-19 vaccination mandates and their lack of concern about the pandemic itself. First, *People's Party of Canada* supporters were the least likely to report getting vaccinated for COVID-19. While 82% of electors overall had been fully vaccinated or intended be vaccinated to when they could, only 28% of PPC supporters were fully vaccinated by the end of 2021. In contrast, 90% of the Liberal Party, 88% of the New Democratic Party, and 80% of Conservative Party supporters had been fully vaccinated or intended to be fully vaccinated as soon as they could. More than half of *People's Party of Canada* supporters (57%) said they would not get vaccinated under any circumstances—51 percentage points more than other electors.

The *People's Party of Canada* was quite successful in attracting the support of unvaccinated Canadians. About 1 in 4 unvaccinated electors said they would vote for the *People's Party of Canada*.

Given that *People's Party of Canada* were far less likely to be vaccinated for COVID-19, they were also more likely to oppose a Canadian government-imposed vaccine mandate on federally regulated transportation workers. While support ranged from 69 to 93% for supporters of the Conservative Party, Liberal Party, New Democratic Party, and Bloc Quebecois, only 11% of *People's Party of Canada* supporters favoured vaccine mandate. 74% were opposed outright.

Opposition to vaccine mandates and vaccinations in general was in part related to the lower levels of concern *People's Party of Canada* supporters had about COVID-19. While 51% of electors were at least somewhat worried about COVID-19 during the 2021 election, only 25% of PPC supporters expressed the same level of concern. In fact, about half of PPC supporters said they were not worried at all about COVID-19, almost 40 percentage points more likely than other electors.

And it was not just opposition to a federal vaccine mandate that upset *People's Party of Canada* supporters. They also believed that the financial support introduced by the Canadian government to support those financially impacted by employment disruptions and shutdowns did not help the economy overall. When asked whether federal government financial support for those impacted by the pandemic has been good or bad for the Canadian economy, only 13% of *People's Party of Canada* supporters thought it had been good for the economy, 40 percentage points less likely than others in the electorate.

It is clear then that the COVID-19 pandemic and anger around vaccine mandates galvanized support for the *People's Party of Canada*. In the 2019 Canadian election, the *People's Party of Canada* received only 1.9% of the popular vote. Two years later, in the midst of a pandemic and with an issue to mobilize support, the party's share of the vote more than doubled to almost 5%. But the COVID-19 pandemic was a proxy issue for the *People's Party of Canada*. Other insights from the surveys find *People's Party of Canada* held views that were quite different from other electors.

For one, *People's Party of Canada* supporters were far less trusting of others than the rest of the electorate. Only 19% of *People's Party of Canada* supporters believed that most people can be trusted, almost thirty percentage points lower than others in the electorate.

People's Party of Canada supporters were far more likely to deny climate change exists and even held completely different perceptions about whether the summer weather in Canada was hotter than normal.

Two-thirds (66%) of *People's Party of Canada* supporters believed the temperatures where they lived during the summer of 2021 were not hotter than usual compared with 65% who believe they *were* hotter than normal.

Finally, there is evidence that the *People's Party of Canada* attracted the support of electors who may have not otherwise voted or participated in politics. When asked who their second choice would be if they did not vote for the *People's Party of Canada*, 39% said they did not have a second choice while 30% favoured the Conservative Party as their second choice. Only 10% would choose the NDP, 6% the Green Party while another 3% said their second choice would be the Liberal Party.

Conclusion

To draw this chapter to a close requires acknowledging the fact that our survey data profiling supporters of the People's Party of Canada revealed a number of key attributes of these Canadians that were clearly related to our broader analysis of protest and anger as motivating or mobilizing factors in politics. The first key attribute centers upon economic grievances among PPC supporters. For example, the aforementioned higher unemployment rate among PPC supporters than other members of the electorate lends itself to fostering resentment and bolsters support for a growing sentiment that contemporary Canadian society has plenty of expanding cracks and that more and more Canadians—PPC voters included—are falling through those cracks. Furthermore, they argue that the political apparatus tends to ignore the Canadians who fall through these cracks in our society. In other words, PPC supporters argue that the economic system is rigged to empower well-connected Canadians at the expense of less-well-connected Canadians. Such a line of reasoning is reminiscent of the themes espoused by Cramer (2016), Hochschild (2018), McQuarrie (2017), Webster (2020), and Webster et al. (2022).

The second key attribute also revealed concerns about grievances but, instead of economic grievances, it primarily concerned social grievances. As the primary data showcased, PPC supporters are inclined to contest the establishment thinking on a variety of ideologically and politically divisive topics ranging from climate change, the role of the state in curtailing personal liberties in the name of public safety and public health, and the number of faith voters should place in both individuals and institutions among other things. The work of Cramer (2016), Hochschild (2018), McQuarrie (2017), Resnick (2000) and Wuthnow (2019) come to mind here.

The third key attribute contends with the all-important perceived trajectory of the country among PPC supporters. Those potential voters are much more likely to argue that Canadian society is moving in the wrong direction and that much of that misguided trajectory is the result of the leadership of establishment politicians—especially Prime Minister Justin Trudeau. In fact, the blame heaped upon Trudeau for the conceived misguidance of the country has become increasingly visceral and, at times, vitriolic. Such a perceived pattern highlights the work of Fukuyama (2018), Linklater (2022), Mishra (2017), Nevitte (1996), and Veroni (2014).

With these three attributes of PPC supporters in mind, the Conservative Party of Canada (CPC) would probably be the natural home to most PPC supporters, but the CPC failed to appeal to them while also appealing to the 80% of Canadians who supported vaccines and still feared the pandemic. And, since the COVID-19 pandemic and especially vaccine mandates aimed to combat COVID became such important and galvanizing motivations for PPC supporters, a few key questions must be asked: without a pandemic, can the PPC still be relevant? Will a possible global recession, deep anxiety about the cost of living, and rising inflation give the PPC further issues to galvanize voters? Or, will the new Conservative Party leader, Pierre Poilievre, erode the PPC's support by speaking to those voters using language that appeals to their grievances and which could bring them into the CPC's camp? There is already evidence that the PPC is losing some of its support. In an Abacus Data poll conducted at the end of January 2023, 1 in 5 *People's Party of Canada* voters from 2021 say they would support the Conservative Party of Canada today if an election was held.

In sum, when we consider the use of protest and anger as motivating or mobilizing factors in politics, especially in current-day Canada, a few lessons can be learned. First, protest parties tend to emerge out of hardship—mostly but not limited to economic hardship. The parties give voice to those affected and provide electoral order to their anger. Second, somewhere along the way, some real or imaginary slights are perceived which act as a catalyst for the formation of a new political party. Third, it appears that internal discord and infighting are important factors in explaining the emergence of protest movements. And finally, charismatic leadership is often involved. In greatly varied ways, H.H Stevens, Réal Caouette, Preston Manning, Lucien Bouchard and now Maxime Bernier were able to connect with disenfranchised voters and successfully tap into their anger.

Table 6.1 Demographic and socio-economic profile of People's Party supporters vs. other electors

	People's Party supporters (%)	Other electors (%)
Aged 45 and under	55	44
Male	64	49
Male and under 45	33	22
Racialized identity	17	20
Born outside of Canada	9	19
Household income under $50,000	46	43
Unemployed (% of working age)	31	7

Source Abacus Data 2021 Election Surveys, $n = 13{,}932$

Table 6.2 Views on the direction of Canada

	People's Party supporters (%)	Other electors (%)
Headed in the right direction	15	38
Off on the wrong track	80	44
Unsure	5	18

Question: Generally speaking, do you think things in Canada are headed in the right direction or are they off on the wrong track?
Source Abacus Data 2021 Election Surveys, $n = 13{,}932$

Table 6.3 Feelings towards Justin Trudeau

	People's Party supporters (%)	Other electors (%)
Positive	6	37
Neutral	11	16
Mostly negative	8	17
Very negative	75	27
Don't know	–	2

Question: Do you have a positive or negative impression of the following people? [Prime Minister Justin Trudeau]
Source Abacus Data 2021 Election Surveys, $n = 13{,}932$

Table 6.4 Position on COVID-19 vaccination

	People's Party supporters (%)	Other electors (%)
Fully vaccinated or intended to be fully vaccinated	28	84
Have had no shots but am ready to get a shot as soon as it is available for me	8	3
Would prefer to wait a bit before taking it	6	5
Prefer not to take it but could be persuaded to	1	2
Will not take it under any circumstances	57	6

Question Which of the following best describes your position on taking a COVID-19 vaccine?
Source Abacus Data 2021 Election Surveys, $n = 13{,}932$

Table 6.5 Support for federal vaccine mandate

	People's Part supporters (%)	Other electors (%)
Support	11	76
Neither	15	10
Oppose	74	13

Question As you might know, airlines, train operators and public transit companies are requiring their staff—pilots, flight attendants, engineers, and drivers—to be fully vaccinated to be able to work Do you generally support or oppose this requirement?
Source Abacus Data 2021 Election Surveys, $n = 13{,}932$

Table 6.6 Trust in other people

	People's Part supporters (%)	Other electors (%)
Most people can be trusted	19	44
You can't be too careful	81	56

Question Generally speaking, would you say that most people can be trusted or that you can't be too careful in dealing with people?
Source Abacus Data 2021 Election Surveys, $n = 13{,}932$

References

Althoff, G. (1998). Ira Regis: Prolegomena to a History of Royal Anger. In B. Rosenwein (Ed.), *Anger's Past: The Social Uses of an Emotion in the Middle Ages* (pp. 59–74). Ithaca, NY: Cornell University Press.

Banzinger, T., & Scherer, K. R. (2005). The Role of Intonation in Emotional Expressions. *Speech Communication*, 46(3–4), 252–267.

Biassoni, F., Balzarotti, S., Giamporcaro M., & Ciceri, R. (2016). Hot or Cold Anger? Verbal and Vocal Expression of Anger While Driving in a Simulated Anger-Provoking Scenario. *SAGE Open*, July–September 2016, 1–10.

Cramer, K. J. (2016). *The Politics of Resentment: Rural Consciousness in Wisconsin and the Rise of Scott Walker*. Chicago, IL: The University of Chicago Press.

Engels, J. (2015). *The Politics of Resentment: A Genealogy*. University Park, PA: The Pennsylvania State University Press.

Fukuyama, F. (2018). *Identity: The Demand for Dignity and the Politics of Resentment*. New York, NY: Picador.

Hochschild, A. R. (2018). *Strangers in Their Own Land: Anger and Mourning on the American Right*. New York, NY: The New Press.

Jaeger, S. C. (1985). *The Origins of Courtliness: Civilizing Trends and the Formation of Courtly Ideas, 939-1210*. Philadelphia, PA: University of Pennsylvania Press.

Laukka, P., Neiberg, D., Forsell, M., Karlsson, I., & Elenius, K. (2011). Expression of Affect in Spontaneous Speech: Acoustic Correlates and Automatic Detection of Irritation and Resignation. *Computer Speech and Language*, 25, 84–104.

LeDuc, L., Pammett, J. H., & Turcotte, A. (2016). *Dynasties and Interludes: Past and Present in Canadian Electoral Politics* (2nd ed.). Toronto, ON: Dundurn Press.

Linklater, A. (2022). Anger and World Politics: How Collective Emotions Shift Over Time. *International Theory*, 6(3), 574–578.

McQuarrie, M. (2017). The Revolt of the Rust Belt: Place and Politics in the Age of Anger. *The British Journal of Sociology*, 61(S1), S120-S152)

Mishra, P. (2017). *Age of Anger: A History of the Present*. New York, NY: Farrar, Straus and Giroux

Nevitte, N. (1996). *The Decline of Deference: Canadian Value Change on Cross-National Perspective*. Peterborough, ON: Broadview Press.

Resnick, P. (2000). *The Politics of Resentment: British Columbia Regionalism and Canadian Unity*. Vancouver, BC: UBC Press.

Veroni, C. (2014). *Spin: How Politics has the Power to Turn Marketing on Its Head*. Toronto, ON: House of Anansi Press Inc.

Webster, S. (2020). *American Rage: How Anger Shapes Our Politics*. Cambridge, UK: Cambridge University Press.

Webster, S. W., Connors, E. C., & Sinclair, B. (2022). The Social Consequences of Political Anger. *The Journal of Politics*, 84(3), 1292–1305.

Wuthnow, R. (2019). *The Left Behind: Decline and Rage in Small-Town America*. Princeton, NJ: Princeton University Press.

CHAPTER 7

The Neglected Populists: Breaking Down the Performance of the Left-Leaning New Democratic Party in the 2021 Canadian Federal Election

André Turcotte and Vincent Raynauld

Abstract Over the past decade, right-wing populist politicians, political parties and protest movements have experienced "relative electoral

Manuscript to be submitted for the edited collection titled "Political Marketing in the 2021 Canadian Federal Elections" edited by Jamie Gillies, Vincent Raynauld, and André Turcotte.

A. Turcotte (✉)
School of Journalism and Communication, Carleton University, Ottawa, ON, Canada
e-mail: andre.turcotte@carleton.ca

V. Raynauld
Department of Communication Studies, Emerson College, Boston, MA, USA
e-mail: vincent_raynauld@emerson.edu

success" by leveraging specific political or policy issues as well as existing public sentiment for political gain. While these phenomena have received significant interdisciplinary scholarly attention internationally, much less work has been conducted on the manifestation of populism on the left of the political spectrum, especially from a political marketing perspective. This chapter addresses this gap in the academic literature by taking an interest in the populist political marketing performance of the left-leaning New Democratic Party of Canada (NDP) and its leader—Jagmeet Singh during the 2021 Canadian federal election. Specifically, it takes a deep dive into how the NDP and its leader leveraged the potential—but fell short—of left-wing populist political markets in order to generate enough public support in order to win the elections. In many ways, this study shows that the untapped potential of its left-wing populist politics deserves more scholarly and professional attention.

Keywords New Democratic Party · Populism · Left-wing politics · NDP · Jagmeet Singh · Political marketing · Political markets

What happened? At the onset of the 2021 Canadian federal election campaign, conditions were optimal for the New Democratic Party of Canada (NDP) and its leader—Jagmeet Singh—to make some electoral gains and alter the structure of the Canadian political landscape. A Navigator study conducted prior to the dropping of the writ[1] revealed that 58% of respondents considered "it was time for a change" in Canada. Moreover, Canadians were split about the direction of the country whereas 51% believed Canada was on the right track while 49% held the opposite view. In many ways, these data points, which echoed the findings of other polls (Angus Reid Institute 2021; Léger 2021), pointed to an uphill battle between incumbent prime minister Justin Trudeau and the Liberal Party of Canada (LPC). The data was also promising for Jagmeet Singh's NDP. Canadian voters appeared to have grown comfortable with Singh who was leading his party into a second federal election since being chosen NDP leader following a vote on October 1, 2017. Indeed, in

---

[1] The online study was conducted with 1825 adult Canadians between August 6 and August 12, 2021. The authors would like to thank Navigator for permission to use the data for this paper.

a subsequent Navigator study,[2] 46% of Canadians were of the belief he would do a good job as prime minister, slightly behind current prime minister Trudeau at 51%, but well ahead of Conservative Party of Canada (CPC) leader Erin O'Toole (30%). More importantly, Singh was especially well positioned to benefit from a populist edge. The same Navigator study showed that 41% of respondents viewed him as the political leader "who understood people like me", ahead of his major-party opponents Trudeau (36%) and O'Toole (24%).

Yet, when the votes were tallied on Election Day, Singh and the NDP failed to capitalize on these conditions and make significant gains. The NDP finished third with 17.8% of the popular vote (3,036,348 votes) (Elections Canada 2021), compared to its fourth place in the 2019 Canadian federal elections—behind the LPC, the CPC, and the Bloc Québécois (BQ)—with 16% of the popular vote (2,903,722 votes) (Elections Canada 2019). While some scholars have taken interest in the outcome of the 2021 federal election from different disciplinary perspectives (e.g., Marland and Giasson 2022; Pammett and Dornan 2022), this chapter looks at the issue through the lens of a phenomenon that has affected several electoral outcomes around the world in the last five years: populism (e.g., Bracciale et al. 2021; Fenoll 2022; Pérez-Curiel et al. 2021).

Right-wing populism has received significant attention in the mainstream press as well as on social media over the last decade (e.g., Maurer et al. 2022; Pérez-Curiel 2020). It has also played a more prominent role in the dynamics of political campaigning—in and out of elections—internationally. Many social scientists have taken notice. They have examined populism-infused political communication, marketing, and organizing strategies that have been developed and utilized by candidates and political organizations in different national contexts (Busby 2022). Among them include Nigel Farage in England (Tindall 2022), Marie Le Pen in France (Soffer 2022), Giorgia Meloni's Brothers of Italy (Martella and Bracciale 2022), Donald Trump in the United States (Raynauld and Turcotte 2022), and Jair Bolsonaro in Brazil (Mangerotti et al. 2022). Populism as a form of voter appeal and engagement has taken off and gained significant traction. Several social, economic, political and media

---

[2] This second online study was conducted with 1513 adult Canadians between August 26 and September 1, 2021. The authors would like to thank Navigator for permission to use the data for this paper.

factors have contributed in varying ways to this trend. For example, the declining trust in media, political and democratic institutions among some segments of the public as well as the growing uses of social media for political outreach and engagement have helped to strengthen and grow the potency and reach of populist appeals (Gerbaudo 2018; Geurkink et al. 2020; Hopster 2021).

In Canada, the merger between the Canadian Alliance—the successor of the Reform Party—and the Progressive Conservative Party of Canada in 2003 dampened populist efforts at the federal level. While newly elected CPC leader Pierre Poilievre appears to want to reignite such efforts (Budd 2020; Elmer et al. 2022), provincial premiers such as Ontario's Doug Ford and Quebec's François Legault have successfully picked up the mantle and leveraged political personalization and injected populism in their political marketing appeals (Bernatchez 2019; Budd 2020; Erl 2021). As noted by Lachapelle and Kiss (2019: 970), "Doug Ford's victory in the 2018 Ontario general provincial election has been widely cited as an example of the global wave of right-wing populism coming of age [...]." This book chapter argues that lost in the emphasis on the right side of the political spectrum is the potential appeal and continued influence of left-wing populism. Away from the spotlight directed towards right-wing populism, there are other examples ensconced in a more leftist tradition.

About a decade ago, inspired by and building on the urge of transnational protest efforts such as the Indignados movement in Spain, the Occupy Wall Street movement emerged in the financial district of New York City and quickly spread to many countries (Calhoun 2013; Castañeda 2012). This protest initiative—which became the international *Occupy* movement and had local and regional offshoots with often specific interests and objectives (Butler 2019; Maguire et al. 2018)—had leftist and populist leanings and implications. Among them include its opposition to social and economic inequalities and its support of more progressive policy priorities. The movement, which coined the slogan "We are the 99%", pinned the public against the social, economic, and political elites—or the 1%—which were presented to be in—some cases—as corrupt and controlling most of the world's wealth (Reinecke 2018).

In the meantime, left-wing populist political parties espousing similar ideologies and objectives made inroads across Europe. In 2015, the political party Syriza, which favoured policy positions favouring LGBTQ+

rights, secularism, and anti-neoliberalism, won the election in Greece. In Spain, Podemos emerged as credible alternatives to the Conservative Party (Garcia Augustin 2020). Also of interest are the electoral performances of France Insoumise, Germany's Die Linke, and Portugal's Bloco de Esquerda. To some extent, UK Labour Leader Jeremy Corbyn's campaign and Bernie Sanders' two unsuccessful attempts to secure the Democratic presidential nomination in the United States can be viewed as other manifestations of the breadth and depth of left-wing populism forces' influence between 2011 and 2022 (Gillies 2017; Penney 2017). More recently, and of particular interest for this chapter, the Nouvelle Union Populaire et Ecologique et Sociale (NUPES) was formed just before the 2022 French legislative elections and constitutes a template of interest for future left-wing populist efforts.

In Canada, the results have been lackluster. In the 2011 federal election, NDP leader Jack Layton, with the help of his left-populist approach featuring "a blend of collectivist, agrarian populism and populist unionism", led his party to a historic performance, winning 103 seats and forming the official opposition party (Medeiros 2021: 992). However, this success was short-lived. The NDP was unable to build on this momentum nor recover from the untimely death of its leader in August 2011. Within a decade, the NDP was relegated to fourth-party status with only 25 seats. Nevertheless, Canada has a long tradition of leftist movements and parties with populist appeals, from the United Farmers of Canada to the Co-operative Commonwealth Federation (CCF) and, to some extent, Quebec's Parti Québécois (Marland and Flanagan 2015; McDonald 2013). These movements make Canada a case of particular interest for the study of left-wing populism.

Relying on two quantitative national studies conducted during the 2021 Canadian federal election, this chapter explores left-wing populist political markets and the extent to which the NDP and its leader Jagmeet Singh had the potential—but fell short—of leveraging the support of those segments of the voting public. In order to do so, this book chapter first offers a review of the literature defining populist movements in general, which was largely focused on its right-wing manifestation but also looks at its left-wing subsegment. It also takes an interest in the conceptualization of populism as a form of political communication and marketing. Second, it spotlights the recent electoral success of the NUPES in the 2022 French legislative election as a potential roadmap for left-wing populist candidates and parties. Those two sections allow for a sorting out of variables conducive to vote gains and point to an analysis of those variables in the 2021 Canadian federal election. This book chapter suggests that while right-wing populism may have crowded out other references, the untapped potential of its left-wing counterpart deserves more attention from both academics and election strategists.

A Worldwide Phenomenon: What We Know About the Recent Rise of Populism

Over the past decade, many right-wing populist parties and politicians have experienced "relative electoral success" internationally (Raynauld and Turcotte 2018). Aside from the more well-known cases discussed previously, other examples help document the scope and depth of this phenomenon's influence. One of the earliest signs of the emergent movement occurred in 1999 when Jörg Haider's Freiheitliche Partei Österreichs (FPÖ) became part of a new coalition government in Austria. Two years later, the Dansk Folkeparti (DF) secured 12% of the popular vote in the 2001 Danish general election. In 2001, the regionalist party Lega Nord (LN) allowed prime minister Silvio Berlusconi to remain in power by joining the governing coalition in Italy. However, it was Marine Le Pen's father who garnered the earliest attention. Jean Marie Le Pen's victory over Socialist prime minister Lionel Jospin in the first round of the 2002 French presidential contest is often cited as a defining moment for European right-wing populism (Norris 2005; Mudde 2007; Art 2011). Le Pen showed the potential of a well-articulated, right-wing populist-infused messaging as well as voter outreach and engagement. In many ways, it inspired leaders and political parties with similar ideological dispositions across Europe.

Following the 2008 global financial crisis, there was a surge in support for right-wing populist forces in heterogeneous environments and contexts across Europe. As Art observes (2011: 239), "one could certainly point to specific election results, such as the British National Party (BNP) breakthrough in the 2009 European Parliament elections, the Party of Freedom's (PVV) 17% in the same contest, and the Movement for a Better Hungary's (Jobbik) 16.7% in the 2010 parliamentary elections" as the apparent consolidation of right-wing populist appeal. Also of note was the emergence of the neoliberal populist Fremskrittspartiet (FrP)—also known as Progress Party—in left-of-centre Norway.

Several explanations have been put forth to clarify right-wing populism's relative successes. Most of them focus on the link between populism and the success of the radical right in many national contexts. In general, it is suggested that "variations in the success of the radical right are attributed to how far parties respond effectively to public demand through their own actions and strategies", which include political messaging (Norris 2005: 15; see also: Mudde 2007; Art 2011). The ability of right-wing populism to tap into and leverage an existing demand and public sentiment for political gain is key to its success. For example, Rydgrens (2008: 737–738) argues that the radical right in Western Europe has become popular among some slices of the political market by embracing outreach and mobilization approaches centred around "a fundamental core of ethno-nationalist xenophobia (based on the so-called 'ethno-pluralist doctrine') and anti-political-establishment populism". Others have focused on the dynamics of electoral competition. In this vein, Kitschelt (1997: vii) points out that "the success of the extreme right is contingent upon the strategic choices of the moderate conservative parties [and more specifically when] moderately left and right parties converge toward the median voter". Arzheimer (2009) and Ivarsflaten (2008) note that one key policy factor defining a radical right party is an unwaveringly conservative stance in matters related to national identity and a firm rejection of multiculturalism. Moreover, such parties are to be understood as "anti-elite parties that campaign on a very strict definition of national interest and national belonging" (Lochocki 2017: 7).

The intermittent rise of the radical right in several European countries can be tied to specific contextual political, economic, and social variables. Norris (2005) pinpoints ten key reasons explaining these permutations:

1. A post-industrial economy;
2. The dissolution of established identities, fragmentation of the culture, multiculturalization;
3. The emergence or growing salience of the sociocultural cleavage dimension;
4. Widespread political discontent and disenchantment;
5. Convergence between the established parties in political space;
6. Popular xenophobia and racism;
7. Economic crisis and unemployment;
8. Reaction against the emergence of New Left and/or Green parties and movements;

9. A proportional voting system;
  10. Experience of a referendum that cuts across the old party cleavages.

Though relevant, Norris' framework is somewhat limited as it only addresses the reasons driving electoral success from a broad perspective. Nevertheless, she summarizes the key variables fueling the emergence and relative electoral success of right-wing populist politics. Polyakova (2015: 63–65) complements Norris' analysis by unpacking the differences between radical right support in Eastern and Western Europe. Through a comparative lens, she identifies the following variables:

 1. Political stability has a greater effect on public support for the radical right in Eastern Europe,
 2. Social factors, especially civic participation, and trust, have little impact on public support for the radical right across Europe,
 3. Economic decline explains the rise of radical right parties, but not continued electoral support,
 4. High immigration and political instability matter more than economics in explaining support for radical right parties,
 5. While economic decline itself does not explain support for radical right parties, the perceived ability—or lack thereof—of their governments to effectively manage the effects of an economic crisis is important.

Lochocki (2017: 62) further builds and expands on this analysis. He suggests that "public support for populist radical parties increases when conservative parties have mobilized on the immigration topic and have dropped their conservative position over the course of the debate". For his part, Art (2011) focuses on the radical right's successes and failures. He supports previous conclusions that the emergence of the radical right can be traced to key contextual variables. Among them include types of electoral systems, specific economic crises and immigration, massive structural transformations, post-industrialization, globalization and European integration (Art 2011). Additionally, he stresses that more attention must be paid to internal factors specific to political parties: "the internal life of radical right parties is shaped by the nature of their activists" (Art 2011: 6). Specifically, he argues that:

Clearly, the internal political dynamics of radical right parties are important for understanding their success and failure. The struggles for power within these parties, the battles between various factions, and **the strategies of leaders and activists** (emphasis added) assume a central role in this book's narrative. These forms of intentional action have been ignored or obscured in most analyses of the radical right, particularly those who view it as the inevitable outgrowth of broad socioeconomic forces. (Art 2011: 232)

One of the neglected dimensions of the analysis of the success of right-wing populism is the dynamic that has led parties on the left side of the spectrum to vacate this ideological space and allow the right to fill the vacuum. Of particular interest is Roberts' work (2018: 145) who takes interest in how "different types of populist leaders and movements reconfigure the competitive alignments of a given democratic order" (see also: Roberts 2019). While some policy areas are arguably ensconced on the right of the political ideology scale, many others have broader—and to some degree mainstream—political market appeal and could have been addressed by left-wing populist political forces. Hence, one must ask why the corresponding lack of success?

One of the explanations is that "populism is [likely more] a discursive strategy of constructing a political frontier dividing society into two camps and calling for the mobilization of the underdog against those in power" than a coherent ideological program (Mouffe 2018: 10–11; see also: Moffitt and Tormey 2014). As Mouffe (2018: 11) suggests, "[i]t is not an ideology nor a political regime. It is a way of doing politics that can take various ideological forms according to both time and place and is compatible with a variety of institutional frameworks". Several scholars echo and build on this point. De Vreese et al. (2018) conceptualize populism as a form of political communication comprising two distinct facets: (1) the content, which refers to "the public communication of core components of populist ideology (such as people-centrism and anti-elitism) with a characteristic set of key messages or frames"; (2) the style, which alludes to "the use of a characteristic set of presentational style elements" (De Vreese et al. 2018: 425). Populism can also serve political marketing objectives as it represents a "political style based on provocations, offensive language, aggressiveness, and negative emotionality" that is used by candidates and organizations to attract attention, differentiate themselves from their opponents, position themselves politically, as well as connect with specific segments of the political market (Nai 2021: 220).

In other words, on top of representing a political ideology framework, populism can be seen as a form of political messaging and marketing appeal—or mass "mediated political performance" with marketing implications—designed to reach out, connect with, and sell specific political products to the public (Ekström et al. 2018; see also: Baldwin-Philippi 2019; Kissas 2020).

In many ways, left-leaning populist political forces seem to have failed to grasp this distinction. Therefore, right-wing populist parties are attacked as "extreme-right" or "neofascist". Liberal critics insult supporters of those parties as lacking in education and sophistication to disqualify them, without recognizing the psychological and emotional triggers responsible for the emergence of right-wing populist parties. Of particular interest is Hillary Clinton's depiction of U.S. voters supporting Donald Trump in the 2016 US Presidential Election as "deplorables" as an illustration of this strategy. While it is the case that some people are comfortable with right-wing reactionary values, many "are attracted to those parties because they feel they are the only ones that care about their problems" and are willing to develop and enact policies to address them (Mouffe 2018: 22).

Left-wing populism centres around the combination of the populist push for expanding representation, higher participation and the left tradition to promote equality and social justice (Garcia Augustin 2020: 10). As was the case for right-wing populism, the 2008 worldwide economic downturn opened opportunities for the left to mobilize voters around the rejection of austerity politics. One of the challenges was to articulate an economic response while focusing on reasserting the importance of social issues. Of particular interest to left-wing populism are ideas about representation, justice and fairness and what Garcia Augustin described as the "ecological question" (Garcia Augustin 2020: 61). It became imperative to articulate policy alternatives and a vision which would recognize the realities of economic suffering while integrating issues that are the core of Left.

Another characteristic of left-wing populism is the apparent struggle affecting many such parties and standing in the way of consistent electoral success. Many left-wing populist parties are torn between doing everything to win elections or staying consistent with their fundamental principles. While right-wing populist parties tend not to make such distinctions, their leftist counterparts often struggle with the quest for power for its own sake. They also hesitate to rally behind a charismatic leader—like many right-wing populist parties have successfully done—and prefer to define themselves as a movement (Kissas 2020). As noted by Kissas (2020: 271), "populist political communication has always been seen as revolving around charismatic leaders, in the sense that charisma plays an indispensable role in mobilizing and unifying the people against a common enemy". Two illustrations in the Canadian context are the decision by Québec Solidaire to have two co-spokespeople or Green Party candidate Elizabeth May's successful attempt to regain the leadership of the party running with a co-leader. Furthermore, such parties appear torn between embracing left-wing populism or simply returning to leftist policies. Those characteristics cannot be generalized or simplified. Not every left-wing populist party experiences this internal turmoil, nor do they always grapple with such division. One recent example of leftist parties uniting and overcoming tendencies for internal electoral sabotage occurred with NUPES in France.

The NUPES Experiment as a Potential Framework

On April 24, 2022, Emmanuel Macron won re-election as French President with 59% of the vote, defeating Marine Le Pen who garnered the support of 41% of voters. This was not dissimilar from a French Presidential election that occurred twenty years earlier when Jacques Chirac defeated Marine Le Pen's father—Jean Marie Le Pen—with 61% of the vote. One difference between 2002 and 2022 was that by 2022, the French Left appeared in disarray. Of immediate concern were the Legislative elections to be held on the following June 12 and June 19 to elect the 577 members of the upcoming 16th National Assembly.

The prospect of giving Macron control of both the presidency and the legislature acted as a catalyst for negotiations among the diverse political formations of the Left. The details and intricacies of the talks are beyond the scope of this chapter. However, from the start, the objective was clear and politically motivated: deny Macron's Ensemble Citoyens a majority in the Assembly. In doing so, the various parties of the Left overcame their reluctance to favour political over ideological objectives. As mentioned above, many left-wing populist parties have underperformed electorally because of this dilemma. By making its political objectives clear, the NUPES—composed of diverse groups from *La France Insoumise, the Parti Socialiste, the Parti Communiste and Europe Ecologie Les Verts*—broke with that tradition.

Another factor contributing to the swift emergence and relative success of the NUPES was that it had a clear standard bearer. Jean-Luc Mélenchon proposed some kind of coalition as far back as December 2021. After failing to secure the presidency—he came in third behind Macron and Le Pen—Mélenchon focused on unifying the Left. Perhaps even more important was the astute reading of the public opinion environment leading to a citizen-focused platform. The NUPES clearly showed that it understood the problems facing ordinary people and offered solutions. Their proposals include an increase in the minimum wage, the lowering of the retirement age to 60, a freeze on the price of necessities and clear policies to deal with the "ecological question". On June 20, 2022, France woke up to a new term describing their government—"la cohabitation". While Macron's *Ensemble!* won the most seats (246), it failed to win a majority. The NUPES came in second (142). Critics were quick to point out that the NUPES did not win the election and gave a mitigated assessment of the experiment. It remains that what the NUPES was able to accomplish in a very short period can be mined for further scrutiny. A clear alignment with the issue environment, a strong political commitment over ideological ambivalence, and leadership were the elements contributing to NUPES quick rise and electoral impact in 2022.

Left-Wing Populists and the 2021 Canadian Federal Election[3]

With a significant proportion of Canadians wanting change (Léger 2021), there was an opening for opposition parties to make vote gains. The opinion environment was offering several options for favourable party positioning. More than one-third (35%) of Canadians mentioned health care as the most important salient issue facing the country, ahead of the economy at 26%. Climate change was third at 15%, followed by affordability (4%), poverty and income inequality (4%), and racism and Indigenous rights (3%) (Table 7.1).

---

[3] The analysis in this section is based on two online quantitative studies. The first one was conducted from August 6 to 12, 2021 with 1852 adult Canadians. The second study was conducted from August 26 to September 1, 2021, with 1513 adult Canadians. Both studies rely on a panel from MARU.

Table 7.1 Most important policy issue

Issue	%
Health care (including COVID)	35
The economy	26
Climate change	15
Affordability	4
Poverty and income inequality	4
Racism and indigenous rights	3
N = 1852	

Note This table only includes a partial list

It was important for Jagmeet Singh and the NDP to establish some level of perceived competence on those key issues and he came up short. For instance, Singh trailed Justin Trudeau, Erin O'Toole, and BQ leader François-Yves Blanchet as the best leaders to handle two important policy issues for the public in the context of an electoral campaign in the midst of the COVID-19 pandemic and which generated significant uncertainty and anxiety among the public: health care and the economy (see chapter by Lalancette and Raynauld). No one leader did well on issues of affordability, poverty, and racism.

Singh was perceived favourably as a leader able to address issues relating to climate change, but only came in second place behind the Green Party (GP) leader Annamie Paul. This policy issue was of particular interest to left-wing populists and offered the most electoral potential for a coalescence of support. Two-thirds of Canadians believed that climate change was either a top priority (30%) or that "our survival depends on addressing it" (36%). At the same time, only 5% of Canadians thought the Liberal government was doing a very good job addressing climate change with another 23% saying it was doing a good job. Three-in-ten Canadians (30%) believed Jagmeet Singh and the NDP would do a better job than Trudeau government compared to only 18% who felt the same way about Erin O'Toole and the Conservative Party. But left-wing populists simply had too many options on climate change. While Singh was ahead of the other leaders, there was enough vote erosion towards the Bloc and the Green Party to lessen the electoral impact of the issue.

While health care and the economy were the most important salient issues, Canadians had a separate set of latent concerns. When asked to choose from a list of issue priorities, 51% of Canadians identified helping to make everyday life more affordable as an urgent priority and 50% mentioned housing affordability. Those two latent concerns had the electoral potential for the NDP and should have dominated their campaign discourse. Of lesser concern to Canadians were corporate greed (only 32% said it was an urgent priority), defending the rights of racial minorities in Canada (28%), and universal childcare (23%). Those issues were featured prominently on by the NDP on the campaign trail. While important, they were more ideological platform planks than issues with electoral potential.

Not every latent issue was potentially favourable to left-wing populists. Canadians were divided on the impact Prime Minister Trudeau had on Canada's stature in world change. Some 30% felt Trudeau had improved Canada's image abroad while 36% held the opposite view. But the divisions fell along regional and generational lines rather than partisan or ideological ones. More likely to believe Trudeau had a positive impact on Canada's international image were Quebecers (39%), GenZers (38%) and those in Atlantic Canada (35%). In contrast, Albertans (55%) and Boomers (39%) were more likely to have the opposite opinion. With regard to Indigenous issues, only 6% felt Prime Minister Trudeau did a good job on that issue but very few Canadians thought Singh or O'Toole could do better.

While voting intentions and issues remain largely stable throughout the election campaign, perceptions of leaders changed significantly. At the onset of the campaign, 43% of Canadians trusted Justin Trudeau, slightly less than Jagmeet Singh (44%), and behind Bloc Leader Blanchet (50%). Erin O'Toole trailed at 26%. Two weeks into the campaign, the level of trust towards Blanchet dropped to 25%, while Trudeau's decreased to 31%. While the level of trust in O'Toole moved slightly up to 29%, Singh's trust level among the public remained stable at 44%, effectively making him the most trusted main party leader. Canadians were also asked to choose words to describe their impression of the three main party leaders. Similar words were used to describe Justin Trudeau and Erin O'Toole—most of which were negative. Comparatively, the most common words associated with Jagmeet Singh were all positive. Specifically, Canadians saw Trudeau as "disappointing" and "inconsistent" while O'Toole was seen as "untrustworthy" and "dull". In contrast, Singh was seen in a positive light with Canadians most likely to view him as someone "who cares", "approachable" and "standing for what is right". As mentioned above, right-wing populist parties do not hesitate to showcase their leaders, even

Table 7.2 Words associated with NDP party leader Jagmeet Singh

Words	%
Cares	27
Approachable	27
Stands up for what is right	25
For Canadians	24
Smart	23
Progressive	23
Confident	21
Understands	20
Believable	20
Capable	19
N = 1852	

Table 7.3 Words associated with LPC party leader Justin Trudeau

Words	%
Disappointing	36
Inconsistent	35
Arrogant	30
Untrustworthy	29
Pompous	27
Weak	26
Liar	26
Youthful	24
Approachable	24
Confident	23
N = 1852	

at the expense of policy priorities. The NDP campaign was reluctant to do so, especially in Quebec and in the Prairies (Tables 7.2, 7.3 and 7.4).

What's Next?

Much has happened since the 2021 Canadian federal election. The worldwide electoral success of right-wing populism has continued. In Italy, Giorgia Meloni became the first female prime minister at the helm of The Brothers of Italy, a party favouring tighter immigration limitations and the empowerment of regular Italians in opposition of the political elites. In Sweden, the Democrats received the second-highest number of

Table 7.4 Words associated with CPC party leader Erin O'Toole

Words	%
Untrustworthy	27
Dull	24
Disappointing	22
Unengaging	22
Arrogant	21
Inconsistent	18
Pompours	17
Weak	16
Liar	15
Capable	13
N = 1852	

votes. In contrast, aside from NUPES, left-wing populist parties continue to struggle. In Canada, the NDP entered into an informal coalition with the ruling Liberals to last until 2025. It is unclear how this will affect the structure of left-wing populist forces in Canada.

In this chapter, we suggest that aside from the sometimes-vitriolic rhetoric of right-wing populist parties, there are fundamental reasons for their success. It starts with a recognition of the populist appeal as a persuasion tool, marketing and political identity performance, or a discursive strategy. Appealing to disaffected segments of the population and demonstrating that one cares about their problems should not be the privy of one side of the population spectrum. Second, the current opinion environment favours expanding representation, participation, equality and social justice, the environment and "bread and butter" issues. Establishing credentials on all those policy fronts is important. A less tangible but important strategy also includes a willingness to win elections; recognizing that only through controlling government can change be implemented. This often means pragmatism over ideological purity, and this can be done through engaging leadership. As mentioned in this chapter, those elements are not restricted to one side of the ideological spectrum. Looking ahead to the next Canadian federal election, it is conceivable that populist appeals will once again be featured prominently in the electoral discourse and marketing outreach. New Conservative leader Pierre Poilievre has already shown signs that he will take up this mantle. However, other politicians could join the fray. At stake is the 54%

of Canadians who, in 2021, could not name one federal political leader who they felt "understood people like me".

References

Angus Reid Institute (2021). Election 44: O'Toole preferred among leaders on economy, but Trudeau bests CPC leader head-to-head. Angus Reid Institute. https://angusreid.org/wp-content/uploads/2021/08/2021.08.19_Federal_Election_Economy.pdf.
Art, D. (2011). *Inside the Radical Right: The Development of Anti-immigrant Parties in Western Europe*. Cambridge, Cambridge University Press.
Arzheimer, K. (2009). Contextual factors and the extreme right vote in western Europe, 1980–2002. *American Journal of Political Science*. 53(2), 259–275.
Baldwin-Philippi, J. (2019). The technological performance of populism. *New Media & Society*, 21(2), 376–397.
Bernatchez, J. (2019). Les élections de 2018 au Québec: un «moment populiste»?. *IdeAs. Idées d'Amériques* (14).
Budd, B. (2020). The people's champ: Doug Ford and neoliberal right-wing populism in the 2018 Ontario provincial election. *Politics and Governance*, 8(1), 171–181.
Busby, R. (2022). Trump, populism and the pandemic. In Gillies, J. (2022). *Political Marketing in the 2020 US Presidential Election*. Cham, Palgrave Macmillan.
Butler, M. (2019). Promises of transparency, promises of participation: On the ambivalent rhetoric of the occupy-movement. In Berger, S. and Owetschkin, D. (Eds.) (2019). *Contested Transparencies, Social Movements and the Public Sphere*. Cham, Palgrave Macmillan.
Bracciale, R., Andretta, M., & Martella, A. (2021). Does populism go viral? How Italian leaders engage citizens through social media. *Information, Communication & Society*, 24(10), 1477–1494.
Calhoun, C. (2013). Occupy Wall Street in perspective. *British Journal of Sociology*, 64(1), 26–38.
Castañeda, E. (2012). The indignados of Spain: A precedent to occupy Wall Street. *Social Movement Studies*, 11(3–4), 309–319.
De Vreese, C. H. et al. (2018). Populism as an expression of political communication content and style: A new perspective. *The International Journal of Press/Politics*, 23(4), 423–438.
Ekström, M., Patrona, M., & Thornborrow, J. (2018). Right-wing populism and the dynamics of style: A discourse-analytic perspective on mediated political performances. *Palgrave Communications*, 4(1), 1–11.

Elections Canada (2019). The forty-third general election 2019: Official voting results. Elections Canada. https://www.elections.ca/res/rep/off/ovr 2019app/51/table8E.html.

Elections Canada (2021). September 20, 2021 general election national results. Elections Canada. https://www.elections.ca/enr/help/national_e.htm.

Elmer, G., Langlois, G., McKelvey, F., & Coulter, N. (2022). Introduction to special section: The mainstreaming of the Canadian alt-right. *Canadian Journal of Communication* (aop), e20220068.

Erl, C. (2021). The people and the nation: The "thick" and the "thin" of right-wing populism in Canada. *Social Science Quarterly*, *102*(1), 107–124.

Fenoll, V. (2022). Political communication on Facebook and populism. The 2019 European Parliament election in Spain. *Communication & Society*, *35*(3), 91–103.

Garcia Agustin, O. (2020). *Left-Wing Populism*. Emerald Publishing.

Gerbaudo, P. (2018). Social media and populism: An elective affinity? *Media, Culture & Society*, *40*(5), 745–753.

Geurkink, B., Zaslove, A., Sluiter, R., & Jacobs, K. (2020). Populist attitudes, political trust, and external political efficacy: old wine in new bottles? *Political Studies*, *68*(1), 247–267.

Gillies, J. (2017). "Feel the Bern": Marketing Bernie Sanders and democratic socialism to primary voters. In Gillies, J. (Ed.) (2017). *Political Marketing in the 2016 US Presidential Election*. Cham, Palgrave Macmillan.

Hopster, J. (2021). Mutual affordances: The dynamics between social media and populism. *Media, Culture & Society*, *43*(3), 551–560.

Ivarsflaten, E. (2008). What unites right-wing populists in western Europe? Re-examining grievance mobilization models in seven successful cases. *Comparative Political Studies*, *41*(1), 3–23.

Kissas, A. (2020). Performative and ideological populism: The case of charismatic leaders on Twitter. *Discourse & Society*, *31*(3), 268–284.

Kitschelt, H. (1997). *The radical right in western Europe: A comparative analysis*. Ann Arbor, MI: Michigan University Press.

Lachapelle, E., & Kiss, S. (2019). Opposition to carbon pricing and right-wing populism: Ontario's 2018 general election. *Environmental Politics*, *28*(5), 970–976.

Léger (2021). Léger North American Tracker: August 2, 2021. Léger. https://2g2ckk18vixp3neolz4b6605-wpengine.netdna-ssl.com/wp-content/uploads/2021/08/Legers-North-American-Tracker-August-2nd-2021_v2.pdf.

Lochocki, T. (2017). *The Rise of Populism in Western Europe: A Media Analysis on Failed Political Messaging*. Springer.

Maguire, E. R., Barak, M., Cross, K., & Lugo, K. (2018). Attitudes among Occupy DC participants about the use of violence against police. *Policing and Society*, *28*(5), 526–540.

Mangerotti, P., Ribeiro, V., & González-Aldea, P. (2022). Populism, Twitter, and political communication: An analysis of Jair Bolsonaro's tweets during the 2018 election campaign. *Brazilian Journalism Research, 17*, 596–627.

Marland, A., & Flanagan, T. (2015). From opposition to government: Party merger as a step on the road to power. *Parliamentary Affairs, 68*(2), 272–290.

Marland, A., & Giasson, T. (Eds.). (2022). *Inside the Local Campaign: Constituency Elections in Canada*. UBC Press.

Martella, A., & Bracciale, R. (2022). Populism and emotions: Italian political leaders' communicative strategies to engage Facebook users. *Innovation: The European Journal of Social Science Research, 35*(1), 65–85.

Maurer, M., Jost, P., Schaaf, M., Sülflow, M., & Kruschinski, S. (2022). How right-wing populists instrumentalize news media: Deliberate provocations, scandalizing media coverage, and public awareness for the Alternative for Germany (AfD). *The International Journal of Press/Politics*, 19401612211072692.

McDonald, R. (2013). "Telford time" and the populist origins of the CCF in British Columbia. *Labour: Journal of Canadian Labour Studies/Le Travail: revue d'Études Ouvrières Canadiennes, 71*, 87–100.

Medeiros, M. (2021). Demand without supply: Populist attitudes without salient supply-side factors of populism. *Canadian Journal of Political Science/Revue canadienne de science politique, 54*(4), 918–938.

Moffitt, B., & Tormey, S. (2014). Rethinking populism: Politics, mediatisation and political style. *Political Studies, 62*(2), 381–397.

Mouffe, C. (2018). *For a Left Populism*. Verso.

Mudde, C. (2007) *Populist radical right parties in Europe*. Cambridge, Cambridge University Press.

Nai, A. (2021). Fear and loathing in populist campaigns? Comparing the communication style of populists and non-populists in elections worldwide. *Journal of Political Marketing, 20*(2), 219–250.

Norris, P. (2005). *Radical Right: Voters and Parties in the Electoral Market*. Cambridge, Cambridge University Press.

Pammett, J. H., & Dornan, C. (2022). *The Canadian Federal Election of 2021*. Montreal, McGill-Queens University Press.

Penney, J. (2017). Social media and citizen participation in "official" and "unofficial" electoral promotion: A structural analysis of the 2016 Bernie Sanders digital campaign. *Journal of communication, 67*(3), 402–423.

Pérez-Curiel, C. (2020). Trend towards extreme right-wing populism on Twitter. An analysis of the influence on leaders, media and users. *Communication & Society*, 175–192.

Pérez-Curiel, C., Rivas-de-Roca, R., & García-Gordillo, M. (2021). Impact of Trump's digital rhetoric on the US elections: A view from worldwide far-right populism. *Social Sciences*, *10*(5), 152.

Polyakova, A. (2015). *The Dark Side of European Integration: Social Foundations and Cultural Determinants of the Rise of Radical Right Movements in Contemporary Europe*. Stuggart, ibidem-Verlag.

Raynauld, V., & Turcotte, A. (2018). 'Different strokes for different folks': Revisiting fragmentation politics in the age of Donald Trump. In Gillies, J. (Ed.) (2018). *Political marketing in the 2016 U.S. presidential election*. New York, Palgrave Macmillan.

Raynauld, V., & Turcotte, A. (2022). Replicating the 2016 'lightning in a bottle' political moment: Biden, Trump, and winning the US presidency. In Gillies, J. (Ed.) (2022). *Political Marketing in the 2020 US Presidential Election*. Cham, Palgrave Macmillan.

Reinecke, J. (2018). Social movements and prefigurative organizing: Confronting entrenched inequalities in occupy London. *Organization Studies*, *39*(9), 1299–1321.

Roberts, K. M. (2018). Left, right, and the populist structuring of political competition. In de la Torre, C. (Ed.) (2018). *Routledge Handbook of Global Populism*. New York, Routledge.

Roberts, K. M. (2019). Bipolar disorders: Varieties of capitalism and populist out-flanking on the left and right. *Polity*, *51*(4), 641–653.

Rydgren, J. (2008). Immigration sceptics, xenophobes or racists? Radical right-wing voting in six West European countries. *European Journal of Political Research*, *47*(6), 737–765.

Soffer, D. (2022). The use of collective memory in the populist messaging of Marine Le Pen. *Journal of European Studies*, *52*(1), 69–78.

Tindall, C. (2022). Populism, culture and class: Articulation and performance in contemporary British populism. *Contemporary Politics*, *28*(2), 121–143.

CHAPTER 8

Identity Marketing During the 2021 Canadian Federal Election

Mireille Lalancette, Angelia Wagner, Karen Bird, and Joanna Everitt

Abstract This chapter addresses the identity marketing strategies of candidates during the 2021 Canadian federal election. Analysing official biographies, we identify the strategies that candidates used to address the immigration status of themselves or their families. We asked the following research questions: How do candidates use immigration in their political marketing? What role do direct and indirect appeals to identity play in

M. Lalancette (✉)
Département de Lettres et Communication Sociale, Université du Québec à Trois-Rivières, Trois-Rivières, QC, Canada
e-mail: mireille.lalancette@uqtr.ca

A. Wagner
Department of Political Science, University of Alberta, Edmonton, AB, Canada
e-mail: angelia@ualberta.ca

K. Bird
Department of Political Science, McMaster University, Hamilton, ON, Canada
e-mail: kbird@mcmaster.ca

© The Author(s), under exclusive license to Springer Nature Switzerland AG 2023
J. Gillies et al. (eds.), *Political Marketing in the 2021 Canadian Federal Election*, Palgrave Studies in Political Marketing and Management,
https://doi.org/10.1007/978-3-031-34404-6_8

how candidates promote themselves? Fuelled by our work on mediatization and personalization of candidates, we take a renewed look at political marketing practices during an election campaign and focus in particular on the under-research dimensions of identity-based uses of political communications in the Canadian context. Overall, our findings reveal that challengers use their immigration stories to demonstrate a commitment to community and country, while incumbents, high-profile individuals, and second- or third-generation Canadians downplay their immigration background in favour of emphasizing their skills and qualifications.

Keywords Identity marketing · Immigration status · Candidate · Mediatization · Personalization

Introduction

During an election campaign, candidates, leaders, and parties mobilize multiple narratives to create a political persona that appeals to voters. Official biographies presented on party and campaign websites are one way to introduce candidates, helping journalists and constituents to analyse and compare party candidates in a giving riding. In the biographies, we can learn about the candidates' credentials, careers, education, awards, and personal life. But as this chapter demonstrates, biographies offer more than a simple account of a candidate's qualifications—they typically contain explanations from the candidate on why they want to become an elected official. In these appeals they discuss their links to the party, their sense of belonging to the country, their attachment to the riding, and their belief about what the party offers voters. On the one hand, Canadians tend to acknowledge the importance of immigration in the national fabric and to view immigrants as making a positive contribution. And yet, immigrant candidates, especially those who are not white, may

---

J. Everitt
Department of History and Politics, University of New Brunswick Saint John, Saint John, NB, Canada
e-mail: jeveritt@unb.ca

face additional challenges promoting their candidacies because they do not embody the white norm of the traditional politician in Canada.

This chapter addresses the marketing tactics of local candidates with immigrant backgrounds during the 2021 Canadian federal election. Based on an analysis of official biographies, we identify the strategies candidates used to address their immigrant backgrounds during an era of election campaigning that calls for personalization and identity-based communications (Lalancette and Tourigny-Koné 2017; Brown-Dean 2019). We are interested in direct and indirect references to their immigration story and identity. Direct references involve candidates explicitly talking about their identities (e.g., being an immigrant or arriving as a refugee), while indirect references address policies of interest or relevance (e.g., immigration and citizenship policies) and groups with whom they share identities and interests (e.g., meeting with an organization helping immigrants). In both instances these references may be expressive, suggesting they reflect the candidates' concerns as part of an identity group, or instrumental, in that they target appeals to same-identity voters or reflect efforts to reduce anxiety among those voters who themselves are not new Canadians.

By taking a qualitative look at candidate communication strategies, we aim to answer the following questions: How do candidates use immigration in their political marketing? What role do direct and indirect appeals to identity play in how candidates promote themselves? Fueled by our research on mediatization, personalization, and leadership, we investigate the political marketing practices of local candidates with immigrant backgrounds running in the 2021 Canadian federal election and, in the process, offer insights into the identity-based uses of political communications by often overlooked local candidates and in the under-studied Canadian context. This chapter also advances our understanding of how digital communications and political marketing are evolving in North America as more diverse individuals seek elected office.

What can we expect in candidate appeals? Whether in an official biography, on social media, or during campaign stops, candidates use storytelling techniques to shape their image and create a connection with voters. Research has shown that political leadership perceptions are not entirely tied to a rational view of politics (Bauer 2020; Goldman 2017; Mazzoleni 2017; Teles 2015). Social characteristics like gender, ethnicity, race and age as well as personal characteristics like charisma, proficiency, honesty, likeability and approachability come into play when voters and journalists evaluate candidates. Candidates thus accentuate certain traits to appear relatable and qualified for office (Arbour 2014).

Candidate marketing strategies contain three elements: personality, competence and engagement in specific causes or issues (Arbour 2014). To theoretically understand and empirically explore political marketing, Ceccobelli and Di Gregorio (2022) propose a model called the *triangle of leadership*. Their model (Fig. 8.1) aims at understanding the success and failure of contemporary political leaders. This model is also relevant for local candidates because they often mimic their party leader's communication approaches, are bound by party discipline (Marland 2020), and typically act as brand ambassadors for the party in their riding (Marland and Wagner 2020). Ceccobelli and Di Gregorio argue that the three dimensions of the triangle of leadership—authenticity, ordinariness and competence—do not compete with each other but rather work in combination as "aspiring leaders should seek to strike a balance between them" (2022: 118). In other words, leaders and candidates strive to project an image of themselves as people who are like voters but who also have specific competencies that make them especially qualified so that voters can put their faith and trust in them. One of the model's drawbacks, however, is that it does not account for identity. How can ethnic-minority candidates with immigrant backgrounds project an image of authenticity, ordinariness, and competence in a country where the qualities of leadership are normally associated with native-born white men? Considering that immigrant candidates constitute a minority of candidates in Canadian elections and that Canada has few examples of successful immigrant politicians,[1] we hypothesize that immigrant candidates might develop unique marketing strategies to highlight their personal and professional qualities in a way that portrays them as legitimate political actors in Canada.

Candidates use storytelling strategies and marketing techniques to emphasize specific qualities and characteristics that demonstrate their ability to be a good political leader: "Political storytelling encompasses wide-ranging communication and engagement activities enabling politicians to develop, refine, and blend personal and public narratives in order to create, maintain, adjust, and strengthen their public image" (Lalancette

---

[1] In 2021, immigrants (foreign-born Canadians) elected to the House of Commons made up 13% of all MPs (44 of 338), and 70% of these are visible minority immigrants (Black and Griffith 2022). https://policyoptions.irpp.org/magazines/january-2022/do-mps-represent-canadas-diversity/.

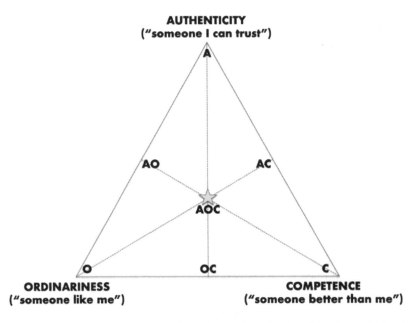

Fig. 8.1 The Triangle of Leadership (*Source* Ceccobelli and Di Gregorio 2022: 118)

and Raynauld 2020: 262–263). These strategies can be discursive by using specific narratives and visuals by creating an imagery that builds the person's political persona. Justin Trudeau has taken this approach to Instagram during his time in office, with posts suggesting he is a reliable leader, good father, international statesperson, and prime minister respectful of minorities and Indigenous peoples (Lalancette and Raynauld 2019; 2020). In short, political storytelling allows politicians to create compelling narratives that attract attention and enable them to bond with voters (Liebhart and Bernhardt 2017; Polletta 2008).

One storytelling strategy is personalization. The candidates not only embody their party's values but also demonstrate their authenticity, ordinariness and competence (Lalancette and Tourigny-Koné 2017; Lalancette and Raynauld 2020). They can also use their private life to humanize their political image. Sharing stories about their upbringing, leisure activities, pets and hobbies enables candidates to claim they have the requisite understanding and experience to legislate on various issues of concern to voters. For example, a politician with children might claim to have caring qualities, a marathoner might argue they have the stamina to put in the long hours demanded of an elected official, and an entrepreneur might suggest their business experience would help them to improve economic policy. These storytelling strategies bring candidates closer to their constituents (Arbour 2014) and are linked to "image management" (Mayer 2004; Marland 2014, 2016).

Extant research on official biographies indicates candidates mostly project a personal image (Herman and Vergeer 2013). Examining websites in the United States and United Kingdom, Stanyer (2008) found politicians promoted qualities such as listening to constituents, being effective managers, and possessing a strong knowledge of issues. In Canada, Cross et al. (2022) find that candidate web biographies in the 2015 and 2019 federal elections focus on candidates' deep community ties, their prior party experience, and their ability to represent their constituency by working on their behalf. Lalancette's (2018) analysis of biographies during the 2012 Quebec election revealed that candidates used storytelling techniques to create a vivid and compelling plea for voter support. Québec Solidaire candidates put their private lives at the centre of their campaigns while Liberal and Parti Québécois candidates seldom did so. When candidates did talk about personal matters, they used their volunteer work and family values to indicate their political skills and potential success in office. All candidates emphasized their links to the territory, regardless of whether or not they lived in the riding, to demonstrate their belonging to the community that they wanted to represent. However, these studies did not examine the role of immigration in candidate storytelling strategies.

The American literature on race and political communication offers some insights into how candidates might discuss immigration in their official biographies, suggesting two strategies in particular. McIlwain (2013) argues that in some contexts, African American politicians might use a racialized distinction strategy whereby they explicitly draw attention to their racial identity to convince voters to support their candidacies. He cites the example of Barack Obama, who wove his life story into the larger American narrative of being a country where everyone, regardless of background, could achieve the American dream through hard work. Obama encouraged all Americans to vote for him as president because it would validate that country's general belief in equality. Broadening this concept to other identity groups, we might expect candidates from other marginalized groups to use an *identity distinction strategy*, whereby they highlight or draw on their particular social characteristics to demonstrate their worthiness for elected office. Following this logic, immigrant candidates might discuss their immigration and citizenship journey to demonstrate their perseverance and commitment to their adopted country.

The American literature on race and political communication identifies an alternative strategy that some candidates might use: deracialization. In this approach, African American candidates minimize their racial difference with voters by downplaying their racial identity and related issues in favour of emphasizing communal issues like the economy (McIlwain 2013; Orey and Ricks 2007). As brothers running for U.S. federal office in 2004, John and Ken Salazar's decision to downplay race in their respective Democratic campaigns was seen as key to attracting white and Republican crossover votes (Juenke and Sampaio 2010). Extending this concept to other identity groups, we might expect candidates to use a *de-identification strategy*, whereby they downplay those social characteristics that mark them as different from the norm in Canadian politics. For example, Muslim candidates might not mention their religious faith or religious organizations because it would indicate they are not Christian.

American theorization of the role of race in political communications pits racial distinction and deracialization as mutually exclusive strategies: candidates cannot use both of them at the same time. The same is not true when candidates possess several identities that they might choose to deploy in campaign communications. Candidates can use an identity distinction strategy for one characteristic (such as immigration) while using a de-identification strategy for another one (such as race). The national context influences which identities are safe to talk about and which ones are not (Doering 2020). The importance of multiculturalism in Canadian society suggests candidates might be comfortable highlighting those aspects of their identity that reaffirm the country's belief that Canada is welcoming to people of all national origins and cultural backgrounds (Beukian 2020). But a general aversion to talking about race in Canada might discourage candidates from highlighting their racial identities. This reluctance could be (temporarily) mitigated by world events, such as the 2020 murder of African American George Floyd by a white police officer, which make race more salient at a given time. This chapter investigates if, and how, Canadian candidates of immigrant backgrounds use these two strategies in their campaign communications.

Methods

This study stems from a larger project exploring the self-presentation strategies of women, Indigenous, racialized, and queer candidates in the 2021 Canadian federal election. To understand how candidates deploy their immigrant identities in political marketing in Canada, we undertook a discourse analysis of the official biographies of 1,142 candidates who ran for the Bloc Québécois, Conservative, Green, Liberal, and New Democratic parties. We excluded candidates who did not provide an official biography or who used a template provided by their party that did not contain any information about them beyond their name. The English- and French-language biographies were retrieved from party and candidate websites during the election. This chapter focuses specifically on the self-presentation strategies of candidates who were born outside Canada as compared to those with an immigrant background.[2]

Official biographies often comprise three to four short paragraphs in which candidates share information about themselves such as their work experience; educational background; volunteer activities; place of birth and arrival to the country or community (if relevant); partner, children, pets and extended family members; personal and political values; and qualifications for elected office. While a photograph of the candidate often accompanies the biography, this chapter does not analyse these visual presentations.

The party-centric nature of Canadian federal politics means individual candidates do not have exclusive control over the content of their campaign messages (Sayers 1999). As brand ambassadors, candidates must promote their party's policy priorities and positions whenever they communicate with voters (Marland and Wagner 2020). But candidates would have control over what information they choose to share about themselves, including social characteristics, qualifications and experiences. We therefore expect official biographies to be an accurate representation of the marketing strategies and storytelling practices of local candidates. Biographies are an opportunity for candidates to help shape their public persona.

---

[2] Because this analysis focuses on candidate websites biographies and how immigrant status is presented in them, it is likely that we underestimate the number of candidates who are new Canadians or second-generation Canadians. If this is the case, the de-identification strategy employed by these candidates is likely to be even more prevalent that our findings suggest.

Results

Our analysis of candidate biographies reveals a striking difference between foreign-born and native-born candidates in how they discuss identity. Foreign-born candidates often emphasized their immigrant identity in the first sentence of their biography, making it central to their public personas. Bloc Québécois candidate Yegor Komarov, who ran unsuccessfully in the Montreal riding of Mont-Royal, played up his ethnic identity to suggest he is both exceptional and ordinary, in keeping with Ceccobelli and Di Gregorio's (2022) trinity of leadership model of communications:

> Yegor Komarov is a Quebecer of Ukrainian origin who immigrated to Quebec in 2004 at the age of five. He has a law degree from the University of Montreal and is a new lawyer. He has lived in Montreal since his arrival and enjoys discovering new aspects of this unique metropolis on a daily basis. (Yegor Komarov, Mont-Royal, Bloc Québécois; our translation)

Immigrant candidates routinely discussed the challenges of their arrival to Canada (i.e., not speaking English or French) and their capacity to overcome differences or disadvantages to successfully integrate into Canadian society. Conservative candidate Indira Bains, who ran unsuccessfully in the Ontario riding of Etobicoke-Lakeshore, presented herself as belonging to Canada after having immigrated from India as a child. She was "shaped" by her community and now wanted to be there for its constituents:

> Indira arrived in Canada with her mom and sister when she was four years old to join her father, who came a few years earlier. They were immediately embraced by their neighbours and their new community. Although she could not speak English when she arrived it didn't stop her from embracing the new community that very much helped shape who she is today. (Indira Bains, Etobicoke-Lakeshore, Conservative)

Her immigrant story is also a success story: she is an accomplished businessperson who has had many important national and international clients:

> As a professional project manager, she manages multi-disciplinary teams to successfully deliver digital, technology and transformation programs on-time and on-budget. Her clients include top Canadian firms such as CIBC, PwC, University of Toronto, Mattamy Homes, Airbus, ABB, Orion

Bus Industries, Origin and Skyservice. (Indira Bains, Etobicoke-Lakeshore, Conservative)

In short, we found many candidates often led off with their immigrant background and in doing so acknowledged it as an important part of their identities. However, many did not employ their immigrant experience to appeal to voters with shared identities. Instead, they followed up this information with details about their accomplishments. This dual approach enabled immigrant candidates to show they were able to overcome obstacles to settle in and become exemplary Canadian citizens in ways that did not position themselves as threats to white English- or French-speaking supporters of their parties.

Leveraging Community

Similarly, immigrant candidates emphasized their roots in the riding. Liberal candidate Soraya Martinez Ferrada, who ran successfully in Hochelaga, presented herself as "a **proud resident** of the east end of Montréal. Originally from Chile, her family settled in the area in the 1980s. Soraya has **deep roots in the community** where she currently resides with her son and daughter" (emphasis ours). Many candidates highlighted the fact that they were longtime residents of their riding who valued their Canadian citizenship. Mohsin Bhuiyan described himself as "a **proud Canadian**, community organizer, successful businessperson, and an **experienced leader**" (emphasis ours). It is only in the second paragraph of his biography that we learn that he was "born in Bangladesh" and "moved to Canada in 1991". Wanting to unseat the Liberal incumbent to become the Conservative MP for Scarborough Southwest in Ontario, Bhuiyan explained that he moved to the riding in 1994 and that he and his wife have lived there for 17 years. The unsuccessful challenger thus used two ways to present his roots in the community. It is also worth noting the formulation of being "born" in a country and not being "from" it and "mov[ing]" rather than coming or being brought to Canada (i.e., as a child). This nuance of language creates a distance from his origin country as it emphasizes the more active or committed choice to become a Canadian.

Another immigrant candidate used the ordinariness of his childhood in the riding as a way to relate to voters. Liberal incumbent Irek Kusmierczyk, who successfully sought re-election in Ontario's Windsor-Tecumseh riding, used his father's work experience to draw a link to the riding's important automobile sector. He also discussed his previous experience as a Windsor city councillor to indicate his knowledge of the riding and its issues:

> **Irek and his family have lived in the Windsor-Tecumseh riding for more than 35 years after immigrating to Canada from Poland.** His father worked in the auto industry and his mom was a teller at a small local credit union. His parents instilled in Irek a passion for community service leading him to a career on Windsor City Council, where he was elected in three consecutive elections. On council, Irek successfully advocated for historic investments in flood protection, road improvements, libraries and parks that improve quality of life. (Irek Kusmierczyk, Windsor-Tecumseh, Liberal; emphasis ours).

Like other candidates (see Cross et al. 2022), immigrant candidates leveraged aspects of their personal history to demonstrate deep roots in and commitment to the community. In this way, they acknowledged their immigrant status while still appealing to native-born Canadian voters who might have felt threatened by it.

Leveraging Immigration

Our analysis of official biographies further indicated that foreign-born candidates often employed their immigration experience to demonstrate they understand the issues in their riding while at the same time embodying the values promoted by their party. Bloc Québécois candidates in particular used their immigration stories to reaffirm the importance of Quebec sovereignty. Anna Somonyan, who ran unsuccessfully in Ahuntsic-Cartierville, linked her Armenian origins to the Québécois identity and the importance of preserving it. Yegor Komarov highlighted his passion for the French language and the need to represent Quebec interests at the federal level.

> A Quebecer by adoption and Armenian by origin, Anna believes in media freedom as a fundamental principle of responsible governance. She is well aware of the challenges of identity preservation and the value of sovereignty. (Anna Simonyan, Ahuntsic-Cartierville, Bloc Québécois; our translation).

Passionate about the French language and concerned about its preservation, he is fluent in three other languages: English, Russian and Ukrainian. A committed citizen, he has been involved in various community activities throughout his academic training in order to contribute to the improvement of the quality of life of his fellow citizens, particularly on issues of access to housing, taxation, as well as assistance to seniors. A newcomer to the world of politics, Yegor joined the Bloc Québécois team because he realizes that it is the only political party in Ottawa that has the interests of Quebecers at heart (Yegor Komarov, Mont-Royal, Bloc Québécois; our translation).

Both immigrant candidates used their life experiences to create a connection with Bloc Québécois values and Québécois identity.

Other candidates viewed their refugee status or immigration journey as a benefit that made them better leaders. Conservative candidate Likky Lavjy, who ran unsuccessfully in British Columbia's Burnaby South riding, credited his refugee experience with teaching him perseverance and hard work. Meanwhile, Liberal candidate Shafqat Ali, who ran successfully in Ontario's Brampton Centre riding, referenced the hardships he endured as an immigrant child to illustrate his commitment to helping constituents.

> **As a Ugandan refugee to Canada, I learned at an early age how to persevere** through many challenges and developed a hard work ethic, a story that is familiar to a lot of immigrants working hard to build a better life for themselves and their families (Likky Lavjy, Burnaby South, Conservative; emphasis ours).
>
> Shafqat is a successful entrepreneur and a proud husband and father of three children. **From humble beginnings to an immigrant success story, he understands what it means to make ends meet**. As the Liberal Candidate for Brampton Centre, Shafqat is committed to being a strong voice in the House of Commons for our community and will fight to ensure you have a better tomorrow. [...] He is running to be your Member of Parliament because he has experienced firsthand how difficult life can be. When Shafqat was 10, he tragically lost his dad who was not only his father but his best friend. His mother raised him on her own as a single mother and he moved to Canada with only a suitcase and a dream to succeed in this beautiful land of opportunity. **Shafqat understands the tremendous opportunities Canada provides**, but also the struggles of a single mother or a university student unable to pay their tuition fees. As your Member

of Parliament, he will focus on moving Brampton Centre forward (Shafqat Ali, Brampton Centre, Liberal; emphasis ours).

As we can see in these excerpts, immigrant candidates insisted that the challenges related to settling in Canada made them stronger and more responsive leaders. An identity distinction strategy, therefore, allowed these immigrant candidates to draw upon multicultural narratives to construct their voter appeals in ways that demonstrated their leadership qualities.

Downplaying Immigration

Not all foreign-born candidates highlighted their immigrant background in their official biographies. In many instances, their migrant story was counterbalanced by accounts of their success in school and at work or, in the case of incumbents, their prior political experience. Conversely, immigrant candidates used a deracialization strategy when it came to race; they rarely talked about their racial identities in their official biographies. The latter finding is surprising considering that many immigrant candidates in the 2021 Canadian election were from racial minority groups and that race became politically salient in the aftermath of the 2020 murder of George Floyd. If racialized candidates were to talk about race during a federal campaign, the 2021 election would have been the best opportunity to do so. That they opted for a multicultural approach to identity-based communications speaks to the socio-political environment and riding demographics in which racialized candidates must operate in Canada.

Liberal incumbent Kamal Khera, who was re-elected in Ontario's Brampton West riding, presented herself as "a first-generation Canadian" who "immigrated to Canada from Delhi, India, at a very young age". Following these affirmations, she explained that "she attended York University where she earned her Bachelors of Science in Psychology with Honours and her Bachelors of Science in Nursing with Honours". References to her immigrant and ethnic identities are counterbalanced by the success story of having graduated with two degrees. But she has another reason to emphasize her education: local voter expectations. Brampton West has a large South Asian immigrant population that places a high value on higher education. By emphasizing her educational accomplishments, Khera positions herself on the exceptional side of the leadership triangle in a way that speaks to many in her constituency.

While the bulk of our analysis focuses on foreign-born candidates, we also examined how candidates who are second- or third-generation descendants of immigrants talked about their identity. Do these candidates feel the same need to focus on their family's migration story, or do they downplay that part of their identity? Our analysis suggests that second- or third-generation Canadian candidates were most likely to opt for the de-identification strategy.

Bloc Québécois challenger Diego Scalzo, the son of an Italian father who ran unsuccessfully in Richmond-Arthabaska, did not mention his family's immigrant background nor other aspects of his identity in his biography:

> Diego Scalzo has been Mayor of the Town of Warwick since 2013. He completed a bachelor's and a master's degree in geography at the Université du Québec à Montréal. For nearly 20 years, he has dedicated his career to community action and has participated in numerous development and consultation committees in the Eastern Townships. He also taught at the Cégep de Victoriaville in the "Mobilization and Development of Local Communities" program. Father of two children, Diego is committed to the environmental and socio-economic issues of his riding as well as the well-being of his fellow citizens. (Diego Scalzo, Richmond-Arthabaska, Bloc Québécois; our translation)

Other second-generation candidates made a point of indicating they were born in Canada. For example, two candidates of Greek heritage played up their Canadian birthplace in their biographies:

> Costas Menegakis is proud to be the Conservative Party of Canada candidate for the riding of Richmond Hill. **He was born in Montreal** and resides in Richmond Hill with his wife Gail and their two children. He is a businessman and entrepreneur, and currently serves as President and CEO of a national marketing and logistics company. (Costas Menegakis, Richmond Hill, Conservative; unsuccessful challenger; emphasis ours)
>
> **Born and raised in Saint-Laurent** [a multi-ethnic riding comprising a city borough of Montreal], Emmanuella Lambropoulos has been proudly representing the people of Saint Laurent in the House of Commons since she was elected in the 2017 by-election. Upon graduating from

McGill University in 2013, Emmanuella began her teaching career teaching History, Geography, as well as Ethics and Religious Culture at multiple high schools on the island, including at Saint-Laurent's Lauren Hill Academy, where she also worked as a resource aid with students who had learning disabilities and autism. (Emmanuella Lambropoulos, St-Laurent, Liberal, re-elected incumbent; emphasis ours)

These candidates' decision to emphasize the fact that they were born and raised in Montreal allowed them to mitigate any doubts about their national origins despite the fact their names distinguished them from so-called "native Quebecers" who trace their ancestry back to France.

Liberal incumbent Adam van Koeverden, son of a Dutch father and Hungarian mother who was re-elected in the Ontario riding of Milton, apparently felt little need to speak to his parents' migration story. As a white man who medaled for Canada at several Summer Olympics, including the all-important gold medal in 2004, van Koeverden had no need to indicate that he was born in Canada. He embodied the (white) warrior masculinity central to norms of political leadership in Western countries. Instead, his personal narrative focused on growing up in riding and becoming an Olympic gold medalist:

> Growing up in Halton, Adam learned from a young age that our community has no shortage of leaders – and that is what he aspires to be. As a World and Olympic kayaking champion, he knows what it means to work hard and achieve results. (Adam Van Koeverden, Milton, Liberal)

In this case, van Koeverden's local origins, Olympic training, and successes can be linked with the triangle of leadership model as being relatable (ordinary), hard-working (authentic), and exceptionally talented (competent). Indeed, this personal history of the local kid rising to become an Olympic champion clearly puts him in the out-of-the-ordinary category.

With name recognition and a public track record, incumbent cabinet ministers might feel less need than other candidates to personalize their family's migration background. Rather than focus on a story of human struggle and perseverance to indicate character attributes that should predict success in elected office, they point to other characteristics and accomplishments that relate more directly to the political responsibilities they have held (Cross et al. 2022). The biographical statement of Liberal incumbent Anita Anand, who was re-elected in Ontario's Oakville riding, is far less intimate than most and never mentioned that she is the daughter of physician parents who immigrated from India. Nevertheless, by pointing to the achievement of being the first Hindu cabinet minister, she distinguished both her extraordinary personal background as well as her federal political experience and competence:

> The Hon. Anita Anand was first elected as Oakville's Liberal Member of Parliament in 2019, and has since served as Canada's Minister of Public Services and Procurement. In this role, she has led Canada through the COVID-19 pandemic on the national effort to supply vaccines, as well as medical and personal protective equipment. Anita is also the **first Canadian of Hindu background** to become a federal cabinet minister. (Anita Anand, Oakville, Liberal; emphasis ours)

These findings indicate that incumbents feel less compelled to address their or their family's immigrant background because they have already served in elected office and have a public record to demonstrate their competencies. Details about their family circumstances and other personal matters are often used to portray themselves as ordinary and relatable, and thus like other Canadians. Since incumbents are a familiar face in politics, they do not have to "dismantle" their difference by describing it as an asset rather than a problem. Our analysis shows that incumbents are more likely to mention their national origins at the end of the biography, thus diminishing the importance of their immigrant background to their public persona. We thus conclude that incumbents use a de-identification strategy when it comes to addressing their personal or family history of immigration to Canada. Like challengers, incumbents are generally silent about their racial identities.

Motivated to Run

Both challengers and incumbents used their experience as immigrants to explain their motivations to run for office. Shola Agboola, the unsuccessful Conservative challenger in Saint Boniface—Saint Vital, attributed his candidacy to a desire to give back to Canada and serve the people of the Winnipeg riding, while Liberal incumbent Sameer Zuberi, who was re-elected in Quebec's Pierrefonds—Dollard riding, wanted to "build bridges" between cultural communities.

Shola's motivation to run for office is his love for Canada. Shola believes Canada has given him and his family so much for which they are grateful. Shola feels a deep obligation to give back to a society that has given hope and opportunities to so many like him. He wants to ensure that new generations of Canadians have the same opportunities and quality of life that he has enjoyed. (Shola Agboola, Saint Boniface–Saint Vital, Conservative)

Sameer Zuberi has been serving the people of Pierrefonds--Dollard as their Member of Parliament since being first elected in 2019. Born and raised in Montreal to a mother of Scottish-Italian heritage and a father who emigrated from South Asia in the 70s, Sameer has worked to build bridges and promote dialogue between Canada's diverse communities from a young age. (Sameer Zuberi, Pierrefonds–Dollard, Liberal)

As we can see in these quotations, both the new immigrant candidate and second-generation candidate present Canada as a generous country to which they want to give back. This approach allows these candidates to present themselves as future MPs who will be there for every community in their riding.

Downplaying Race

Candidates were comfortable mentioning their immigrant background to varying degrees, but they usually avoided direct references to their racial identity in their official biographies. A candidate's racial identity had to be inferred from indirect references. Nadeem Akbar, the unsuccessful Conservative challenger in the ethnically diverse riding of Milton, did not explicitly mention his immigrant background or origins. Nevertheless, his biography included a subtle reference to cricket, a popular sport in South Asian communities:

A loving husband and father or three, **he enjoys cricket with his friends**, soccer with his weekend league team, and he also loves to explore new music with his children in his free time. Nadeem Akbar is a trusted community leader, who will effectively represent every Miltonian, to ensure that we emerge from this pandemic stronger than ever before. (Nadeem Akbar, Milton, Conservative; emphasis ours)

Readers might discern Akbar's racial identity from his name and if they knew cricket was popular among South Asians. Immigrant candidates' decision to use a deracialization strategy in their biographical statements corroborates findings from a separate analysis of how Black candidates discussed identity on Twitter during the 2021 Canadian election (Wagner et al. 2022). Black candidates usually downplayed their racial identities in favour of praising the various ethnic and cultural groups in their riding, which Doering (2020) calls "multicultural moments". Together these results support our contention that minority candidates feel safe describing those aspects of their identities that conform with the country's positive narrative of multiculturalism but downplay those aspects that are seen as divisive in Canada.

Conclusion

An analysis of the official biographies of 1,142 candidates who ran for the major political parties in the 2021 Canadian election suggests differences between immigrant/native-born candidates and incumbent/challenger immigrant candidates in how they addressed identity in their political marketing. Foreign-born candidates, and especially challengers, used an identity distinction strategy that framed their immigration to Canada and the subsequent challenges they experienced as giving them the skills, knowledge, and patriotism necessary to be effective MPs. They would make good political leaders *because* of their immigrant background, not in spite of it. At the same time, an acknowledgement of their immigrant identities was often communicated in ways that reinforced their alignment with their parties' or their communities' values, thereby minimizing fears that they challenged traditional Canadian values or mores.

Immigrant incumbents and native-born candidates whose families had immigrated to Canada appeared to feel no need to address their citizenship status. Rather, they tended to downplay this information in their narratives, opting instead to highlight their skills, experience, qualifications and accomplishments. Incumbents were more likely to use a de-identification strategy because they could point to a record in public office that could demonstrate their competence. Personal information like their favourite hobbies were mainly shared to show how ordinary and relatable they were. Moreover, racialized candidates with an immigrant background usually did not explicitly mention their racial identity, but sometimes it could be inferred from their names and references to personal activities. These implied references to their racialized identities provided subtle cues to voters in their ridings who shared their identity without drawing the attention of those constituents who did not.

Together these findings indicate that, with some variation, immigrant candidates tend to use a combination of identity distinction and de-identification strategies in their political marketing. We assume these are calculated decisions about which social identities to highlight and which ones to downplay, and our analysis suggests such decisions vary in relation to the nature of the ridings in which they run, candidates' incumbency status, their degree of prior political experience, and whether they are foreign-born or descendants of immigrants. To the extent that candidates' biographies focused on their immigration story, this was invariably counterbalanced with accounts of professional and educational accomplishments, prior political experiences, and personal circumstances to craft a public persona that conforms to Canadian expectations regarding the ideal political leader.

References

Arbour, B. 2014. *Candidate-Centered Campaigns. Political Messages, Winning Personalities, and Personal Appeals*. New York: Palgrave Macmillan.

Brown-Dean, K. L. 2019. *Identity Politics in the United States*. New York: Polity Press.

Bauer, N. M. 2020. Shifting standards: How voters evaluate the qualifications of female and male candidates. *Journal of Politics* 82(1): 1–12. https://doi.org/10.1086/705817

Beukian, S. 2020. Gender, sexuality, and nationalism in Canada: A critical reading. In *The Palgrave Handbook of Gender, Sexuality, and Canadian Politics*, eds. Manon Tremblay and Joanna Everitt, 79–100. Cham, Switzerland: Palgrave Macmillan. https://doi.org/10.1007/978-3-030-49240-3_5

Black, J. H. and A. Griffith. 2022. Do MPs represent Canada's diversity? *Policy Options* January 7, 2022. https://policyoptions.irpp.org/magazines/january-2022/do-mps-represent-canadas-diversity/

Ceccobelli, D. and L. Di Gregorio. 2022. The triangle of leadership. Authenticity, competence and ordinariness in political marketing. *Journal of Political Marketing* 21(2): 113–125. https://doi.org/10.1080/15377857.2022.2060644

Cross, W., Pruysers, S. and R. Currie-Wood. 2022. *The Political Party in Canada*. Vancouver: UBC Press.

Doering, J. 2020. Ethno-racial appeals and the production of political capital: Evidence from Chicago and Toronto. *Urban Affairs Review* 56(4): 1053–1085. https://doi.org/10.1177/1078087419833184

Goldman, S. K. 2017. Explaining white opposition to black political leadership: The role of fear of racial favoritism. *Political Psychology* 38(5): 721–739.

Hermans, L. and M. Vergeer. 2013. Personalization in E-campaigning: A Cross-national Comparison of Personalization Strategies Used on Candidate Websites of 17 Countries in EP Elections 2009. *New Media Society* 5(1): 72–92.

Juenke, E. G. and A. C. Sampaio. 2010. Deracialization and Latino politics: The Case of the Salazar Brothers in Colorado. *Political Research Quarterly* 63(1): 43–54. https://doi.org/10.1177/1065912908327229

Lalancette, M. 2018. Les web-mises en scène des candidats aux élections québécoises de 2012: entre discrétion et confession. *Politique et société* 37(2): 47–81. https://doi.org/10.7202/1048876ar

Lalancette, M. and V. Raynauld. 2019. The power of political image: Justin Trudeau, Instagram, and celebrity politics. *American Behavioral Scientist* 63(7): 888–924. https://doi.org/10.1177/0002764217744838

Lalancette, M. and V. Raynauld. 2020. Politicking and visual framing on Instagram: A look at the portrayal of the leadership of Canada's Justin Trudeau. *Canadian Studies* 89: 257–290. https://doi.org/10.4000/eccs.4273

Lalancette, M. and S. Tourigny-Koné. 2017. 24 Seven videostyle: Blurring the lines and building strong leadership. In *Permanent Campaigning in Canada*, eds. A. Marland, T. Giasson, and A. Lennox Esselment, 259–277. Vancouver: UBC Press.

Liebhart, K. and P. Bernhardt. 2017. Political storytelling on Instagram: Key aspects of Alexander Van der Bellen's successful 2016 presidential election campaign. *Media and Communication* 5(4): 15–25. https://doi.org/10.17645/mac.v5i4.1062

Marland, A. 2014. The branding of a prime minister: Digital information subsidies and the image management of Stephen Harper. In *Political Communication in Canada. Meet the Press and Tweet the Rest*, eds. A. Marland, T. Giasson, and T. Small, 55–73. Vancouver: University of British Columbia Press.

Marland, A. 2016. *Brand Command: Canadian Politics and Democracy in the Age of Message Control*. Vancouver: UBC Press.

Marland, A.. 2020. *Whipped: Party Discipline in Canada*. Vancouver: UBC Press.

Marland, A. and A. Wagner. 2020. Scripted messengers: How party discipline and branding turn election candidates and legislators into brand ambassadors. *Journal of Political Marketing* 19(1/2): 54–73. https://doi.org/10.1080/15377857.2019.1658022

Mayer, J. D. 2004. The presidency and image management: Discipline in pursuit of illusion. *Presidential Studies Quarterly* 34(3): 620–631.

Mazzoleni, G. 2017. Changes in contemporary communication ecosystems ask for a "new look" at the concept of mediatisation. *Javnost—The Public* 24(2): 136–145. https://doi.org/10.1080/13183222.2017.1290743

McIlwain, C. 2013. From deracialization to racial distinction: Interpreting Obama's successful racial narrative. *Social Semiotics* 23(1): 119–145. https://doi.org/10.1080/10350330.2012.707039

Orey, Bé D. and B. E. Ricks. 2007. A systematic analysis of the deracialization concept. In *The Expanding Boundaries of Black Politics*, ed. Georgia A. Persons, 325–334. New York: Routledge. https://doi.org/10.4324/9781315131924

Polletta, F. 2008. Storytelling in politics. *Contexts* 7(4): 26–31.

Sayers, A. 1999. *Parties, candidates, and constituency campaigns in Canadian elections*. Vancouver: UBC Press.

Stanyer, J. 2008. Elected representatives, online self-presentation and the personal vote: Party, personality and webstyles in the United States and United Kingdom. *Information, Community and Society* 11(3): 414–432. https://doi.org/10.1080/13691180802025681

Teles, F. 2015. The distinctiveness of democratic political leadership. *Political Studies Review* 13(1): 22–36. https://doi.org/10.1111/1478-9302.12029

Wagner, A., Bird, K. Everitt, J. and M. Lalancette. 2022. Holding back the race card: Black candidates, Twitter, and the 2021 Canadian election. Prairie Political Science Association conference, Banff, Alberta, September 16–18.

CHAPTER 9

Conclusion: The Calm Before the Storm

Jamie Gillies, André Turcotte, and Vincent Raynauld

Abstract This concluding chapter summarizes many of the lessons learned from the political marketing experiences in the 2021 Canadian election. It considers how practitioners might apply these themes for future elections and why branding and marketing continue to be central to political strategy.

Keywords Trudeau · Political branding · Political marketing · Canadian party system · Populism

---

J. Gillies (✉)
Department of Journalism and Communications, St. Thomas University, Fredericton, NB, Canada
e-mail: jgillies@stu.ca

A. Turcotte
School of Journalism and Communication, Carleton University, Ottawa, ON, Canada
e-mail: andre.turcotte@carleton.ca

V. Raynauld
Department of Communication Studies, Emerson College, Boston, MA, USA
e-mail: vincent_raynauld@emerson.edu

© The Author(s), under exclusive license to Springer Nature Switzerland AG 2023
J. Gillies et al. (eds.), *Political Marketing in the 2021 Canadian Federal Election*, Palgrave Studies in Political Marketing and Management, https://doi.org/10.1007/978-3-031-34404-6_9

Like the 2019 federal election, Canada awoke to another Justin Trudeau-led minority government on the morning of September 21, 2021. And like the election just two years earlier, political marketing and branding strategies unfurled a number of innovative ways parties and leaders tried to make appeals to voters. Some were successfully deployed, most notably Trudeau's shift from a personal brand marketing approach to one focused on the weaknesses of the other parties. Some were not so successful like O'Toole's attempt to build a big-tent centrist Conservative Party that did not seem to have the endorsement of the party's grassroots and base. Others, like the NDP and Bloc Québécois, were a mixed bag in terms of political marketing, staving off irrelevance or maintaining a niche with the electorate. The People's Party also showed that marketing to the politics of anger could be successful insofar as splitting some of the right-wing vote. But 2021, despite some of these marketing innovations seen elsewhere, most notably in the 2020 U.S. presidential election, really was Canada's "calm before the storm" election. Pierre Poilievre, recognizing the failures of O'Toole to capture the moment in 2021 and take advantage of a fading brand like Trudeau's, fully embraced that anger politics that drove the People's Party to 5% in the polls. Poilievre, like O'Toole, wants a big tent CPC but he wants to capture the far right as well.

The lessons learned then from the 2021 election campaign are indicative of many Western democracies confronting the mainstreaming of populism from the right and the left as well as incorporating crisis political marketing into the mix. Canada has consistently been a centre-left social democracy, with a majority of voters still supportive of both government's role in the Canadian economy and society. But we are not immune to the forces of frustration that then manifest into the politics of anger. The aftermath of the Canadian election, with widespread demonstrations and trucker protests in early 2022, looked awfully familiar to those observing what had happened in Washington D.C. in early 2021. They also looked eerily similar to the January 2023 protests in Brazil. Populism and extremism have come to Canada and are likely to be mainstreamed into our national politics. The election of Danielle Smith as leader of the United Conservative Party in the province of Alberta is indicative of what is on the horizon. Parties that allow off-centre and far-right elements inside their tent are finding that even within one election cycle, the tail starts to wag the dog. In that respect, the 2021 Canadian election can be seen as the last stand of innocence with a politics of policy debate and ideas, as opposed to an ideological polarization of anger and hostility where politics is a blood sport. This election then mirrors the 2012 U.S. presidential election between Barack Obama and Mitt Romney. That was the last subdued affair of political marketing and branding in the U.S. 2021 is likely the last in Canada for a couple of election cycles.

In this edited collection, we have focused on several key elements in political marketing and branding that made the 2021 election notable. Jennifer Lees-Marshment and Salma Malik point out that while Justin Trudeau's image has fallen in terms of the Canadian population, his support has remained relatively stable. Trudeau was able to position himself as the most effective leader in response to the pandemic and deployed, relatively successfully, a crisis brand management that worked just enough to hang on to a minority government. As Gillies and Wisniewski, as well as Raynauld and Lalancette suggest, Erin O'Toole's attempts to build an image as a middle of the road problem solver and "the man with the plan" did not resonate. Trudeau essentially beat O'Toole, as he did Andrew Scheer, in terms of policy-oriented political marketing. Interestingly, Québec has reverted to a pre-Stephen Harper soft sovereigntist branding, led not so much by the Bloc leader Yves-François Blanchet, but by the popular premier François Legault, who, as Guy Lachapelle points out, essentially operated as the unofficial leader of Team Québec and helped to frame the branding in the province as one centred around not leaders or parties but the province's identity aspirations vis-à-vis the federal government in Ottawa. The NDP, in trying to break out of its return to the social conscience of Parliament role it mined during the Ed Broadbent, Audrey MacLachlan, Alexa McDonough and Jack Layton years, saw Jagmeet Singh attempt to embrace some of the left-wing populism, especially around the cost of living and the environment, with mixed success. While the Greens have been relegated to the sidelines, the NDP was unable to harness a widespread progressive movement positioned to replace the Liberals as a government in waiting.

Trudeau, O'Toole and Singh all attempted brand renewals in this election and each was unsuccessful insofar as changing the basic narrative and dynamics of the campaign. The anti-Trudeau branding the CPC has been pushing since 2013 shifted slightly to brand O'Toole as a positive and competent alternative to Trudeau. Not only was this unsuccessful, Pierre Poilievre immediately returned the party to the anti-Trudeau branding, linking the CPC to the more extreme "F*CK Trudeau" branding of many People's Party supporters and prairie conservatives. As Turcotte, Coletto and Vodrey show in their chapter on the People's Party, the politics of anger can be harnessed as an increasingly motivated voting bloc. Maxime Bernier did just that in 2021 with little money or party organization. Poilievre will certainly try to go after that vote next time. This is likely to lead to more confrontational marketing and branding strategies in the next federal election.

Individual candidates also utilized interesting marketing and branding techniques, something which Lalancette, Wagner, Bird and Everitt explore in the final chapter looking at identity marketing through the lens of immigration and how those personal narratives helped and hindered candidates running for office in 2021. That separation between challengers and incumbents where those trying to win play up their identity in social media while those trying to get re-elected downplay ethnicity and cultural and social identification with communities suggests that political marketing at the local candidate level is thriving alongside party/leader marketing and branding.

Like our 2019 edited collection, this book continues the examination of political marketing and a more traditional look at electoral behaviour. The 2021 Canadian federal election shows that elections matter and framing how leaders and parties' brand and market matter just as much. It would be interesting to investigate further how political marketing is playing out at the sub-party level, as Lalancette et al. look at here with respect to immigration status and social media. This type of research also demonstrates that electoral studies and political marketing should be more inextricably linked and that future studies really need both lenses to explain campaign dynamics and how and why the public is motivated to vote.

In describing the 1997 Canadian election, in which Jean Chrétien and the Liberal Party cruised to yet another majority government, Neil Nevitte, Andre Blais, Elisabeth Gidengil and Richard Nadeau suggested Canada was entering or morphing into a fourth party system (Nevittee et al. 2000). That certainly came to pass as the Reform Party, under Preston Manning, formed the official opposition, the regionalism of our elections became more delineated and ultimately led to the unite the right movement and the election of Stephen Harper and the CPC for three consecutive elections. The third party system, as Meisel described, was "characterized by the preoccupation of the major parties with questions of national unity, particularly relations between Quebec and the rest of the country; the presence of mainly regionally-based minor parties responsible for periodic minority governments; and policy-making in which officials played an increasingly powerful and visible role" (Meisel 2001, 426). Some of those characteristics extended over into the fourth party system as well but one marked change was noted by Bickerton, Gagnon and Smith, in that "new ties of partisanship now bind ... voters to recently created parties...that are more regional and ideological in their appeal. These shifts have increased the balkanization of the Canadian electorate and party system. The divisions between parties and voters have been magnified and multiplied regional bases of party support are more sharply delineated; and the pattern of voter loyalties and preferences is more spatially differentiated (Bickerton et al. 1999)". The fourth party system, marked by more regionalism, lacked the pan-Canadian politics of the era of shared cost programs and constitutional patriation (Carty et al. 2000, 2001). Brad Walchuk, writing in 2012, suggested that the 2003 election represented a turning point as well, a potential fifth party system in which partisan electoral competition was enhanced, social media and the Internet began to play a major role, and policies catered to the whims and wants of a growing and striving suburban middle class (Walchuk 2012). But perhaps this was simply too early an assessment in that the 2015 election shifted us back to the similar dynamics of the fourth party system.

Based on the increasing role of political marketing and the harnessing of new media, Canada may be in a fifth party system now, as the tools of political marketing continue to contribute to destabilizing our party system in its present form. We suggest that while those regional cleavages still exist in Canada and much of the fourth party system remains at least underpinning those electoral and political dynamics, one of the major changes has been how parties and leaders, and individual politicians at the local level, use the tools of political marketing and branding to offer new and potentially destabilizing political discourses while in government, campaigning during the writ period, or as part of the permanent campaign. Further, after years when majority governments were the norm, we now seem to be unable to elect majorities anymore. Harper got one and Trudeau got one but since Paul Martin, the minority government has become the new norm in Canadian politics.

It is political marketing that is leading the changes away from the stability of the fourth party system. Marketing is all about shaving off and destabilizing market share. If we agree that Canadian political parties are now adopting marketing and branding practices that have become commonplace around the post-industrial world, why would we expect anything different than tribal marketing, rebranding and market competition? It is that rationale, while not an absolute certainty, that makes the 2021 election the clam before the storm. Canadians have yet to experience the kind of anger populism centralized in the campaigns of the two major parties. We suggest that this is about to change. Whether we enter an era of the kind of emotional, reactionary and populist political marketing and branding we see elsewhere, or whether our more fragile Canadian political sensitivities recoil at unabashed polarized anger politics, remains to be seen. But the ascendancy of a Pierre Poilievre-led CPC, defiantly right-wing with elements of "freedom"-led rhetorical populism, and with political marketing increasingly incorporating the politics of anger and extremism, likely suggests that the next election could be a true fifth party system in Canada.

References

Bickerton, James, Alain-G. Gagnon, Patrick J. Smith. 1999. *Ties That Bind: Parties and Voters in Canada*. Don Mills: Oxford University Press.

Carty, R. Kenneth, William Cross and Lisa Young. 2000. *Rebuilding Canadian Party Politics*. Vancouver: University of British Columbia Press.

Carty, R. Kenneth, William Cross and Lisa Young. 2001. "Building a Fourth Canadian Party System." *Party Politics in Canada*, eds. Hugh G. Thorburn and Alan Whitehorn. Toronto: Prentice Hall, 2001: 33–35.

Meisel, John. 2001. "Review: Fashioning the Fourth Party System: Canada 1993, 1997, 2000." *Government and Opposition*, 36:3 (Summer 2001), 423–435.

Nevitte, Neil, André Blais, Elisabeth Gidengil and Richard Nadeau. 2000. *Unsteady State: The 1997 Canadian Federal Election*. Don Mills: Oxford University Press.

Walchuk, Brad. 2012. "A Whole New Ballgame: The Rise of Canada's Fifth Party System," *American Review of Canadian Studies*, 42:3, 418–434.

Correction to: The People's Party of Canada and the Appeal of Anger Politics

André Turcotte, David Coletto, and Simon Vodrey

Correction to:
J. Gillies et al. (eds.), *Political Marketing in the 2021 Canadian Federal Election*, Palgrave Studies in Political Marketing and Management, https://doi.org/10.1007/978-3-031-34404-6_6

The original version of this chapter was inadvertently published with the misspelled author name Simon 'Vodry' instead of Simon 'Vodrey' in Chapter 6, which has now been corrected. The chapter has been updated with the change.

The updated version of this chapter can be found at
https://doi.org/10.1007/978-3-031-34404-6_6

© The Author(s), under exclusive license to Springer Nature Switzerland AG 2023
J. Gillies et al. (eds.), *Political Marketing in the 2021 Canadian Federal Election*, Palgrave Studies in Political Marketing and Management, https://doi.org/10.1007/978-3-031-34404-6_10

Index

A
anger politics, 6, 93, 102, 156, 160

B
brand effectiveness, 12, 14
branding
   Erin O'Toole, 2–6, 17, 28–36, 45, 46, 51–54, 56, 64, 65, 156, 157
   François Legault, 2, 157
   Jagmeet Singh, 2, 51, 157
   Justin Trudeau, 5, 6, 10–12, 14, 15, 17–20, 26, 27, 29–34, 36, 50, 51, 65, 156, 157, 159
   Maxime Bernier, 3, 6, 26–28, 34, 35, 158
   Yves-François Blanchet, 6, 157
brand personality, 12

C
climate change, 12, 15–20, 30, 83, 84, 100, 105, 106, 124, 125
COVID-19 pandemic, 2, 10, 20, 44, 46, 56, 104, 105, 107, 125, 148
crisis politics, 5, 156

D
digital marketing, 6

E
economy, 12, 18, 43, 44, 56, 105, 119, 124, 125, 139, 156

F
Freedom Convoy protests, 5

H
hyper-masculine political communication, 6

I
identity marketing, 7, 46, 47, 49, 65, 158

© The Editor(s) (if applicable) and The Author(s), under exclusive license to Springer Nature Switzerland AG 2023
J. Gillies et al. (eds.), *Political Marketing in the 2021 Canadian Federal Election*, Palgrave Studies in Political Marketing and Management,
https://doi.org/10.1007/978-3-031-34404-6

immigration, 7, 27, 77, 82, 98, 100, 120, 127, 134, 135, 138, 139, 143–145, 148, 150, 151, 158

M
marketing strategies
  O'Toole 2021 campaign, 54, 56
  Trudeau 2019 campaign, 26, 27
messaging, 6, 30, 31, 35, 36, 47, 48, 51, 56, 118, 119, 122

P
policy branding, 17
polling, 4–6, 18, 19, 30, 32, 93
populism, 5–7, 34, 36, 115–119, 121–123, 127, 156, 157, 160
  left-wing, 116, 117, 121–123, 125, 126, 128
  right-wing, 5, 115, 116, 118–123, 126–128
public opinion, 124

Q
Quebec nationalism, 84, 87, 102

R
rebranding, 18, 31–34, 36
resentment, 86, 93–97, 99, 101, 106

S
social media, 6, 43, 46, 50, 54, 115, 116, 135, 158, 159

V
voters, 2, 3, 5–7, 10, 12, 13, 15, 18–20, 27–30, 32–36, 43–47, 56, 74–77, 79, 82, 84–87, 92–94, 96, 98, 100–103, 106–108, 114, 122, 123, 134–140, 142, 143, 150, 156, 159
  Quebec, 3, 76, 77, 79, 82, 85–87
vote targeting, 3, 27

Printed in the United States
by Baker & Taylor Publisher Services